RUGBY TOWN

RUGBY TOWN

THE SPORTING HISTORY OF D4

KURT KULLMANN

The
History
Press
Ireland

For Catherine

First published 2016

The History Press Ireland
50 City Quay
Dublin 2
Ireland
www.thehistorypress.ie

The History Press Ireland is a member of Publishing Ireland,
the Irish book publishers' association.

© Kurt Kullmann, 2016

The right of Kurt Kullmann to be identified as the Author
of this work has been asserted in accordance with the
Copyright, Designs and Patents Act 1988.

British Library Cataloguing in Publication Data.
A catalogue record for this book is available from the British
Library.

ISBN 978 1 84588 231 0

Typesetting and origination by The History Press

Contents

Acknowledgments

I have to thank the Ballsbridge, Donnybrook and Sandymount Historical Society for the idea of researching sport and its history in Dublin 4. Once I had made up my mind to look into this, it was my wife Catherine who kept encouraging me. As she grew up in Sandymount, she was able to help me further by sharing her memories. Discussing drafts with her was always helpful and often led to further areas to be researched. She was also a great help when it came to editing and proofreading. Without her there would only be half a book and without her editing and proofreading this 'half-book' would be much more difficult to read.

Many of the sport clubs – especially the bigger ones – have sections about their history on their websites which proved a rich source for information. Some clubs published books for their centenary which were very helpful.

Many past and present club members patiently answered my questions and supplied me with photographs. I express my heartfelt thanks to John Callanan (Wanderers FC); Michael Graham, Donal Lennon and Chris Reid (Lansdowne FC); Barbara Culleton (Bective Rangers FC); Ian Canlon (Monkstown FC); Ken Richardson (Old Wesley RFC); Martin Cowley (Railway Union sport clubs); Kirstin Smith (Railway Union RFC); Niall Pelly (Old Belvedere RFC); Guy Easterby (Leinster Rugby); Kenny Carroll (Railway Union HC and CC), Stephen Findlater (www.hookhockey.com), Gerard Siggins (cricket in general and Lansdowne Stadium), Douglas Clark (Pembroke CC and Railway Union HC); Oliver Rye and Alan Little (Merrion CC); Derek Carroll and Francis X. Carty (Railway Union CC) – the latter also gave useful information about Railway Union in general; Shay Conolly (Clanna Gael-Fontenoy GAC); Noel C. Sands (Shelbourne FC); Robert Goggins (Shamrock Rovers FC); Stephen Mooney (Pearse Rangers FC);

David Nolan (St Patrick's CYFC); Mary Harvey, Grace Comerford and Louise Carmody (Lansdowne LTC); Derek Collins and Frances Walsh (Claremont RU LTC); A. McCormack (Elm Park Golf and Sports Club); Robert Barklie (Herbert Park Croquet Club); Brendan R. O'Donoghue (Neptune Rowing Club); David Doyle and Gerry Brannocks (Stella Maris RC); Philip Murphy (St Patrick's RC); Clodagh Cullen (Poolbeg Yacht and Boat Club); Ciarán Kirwan (boxing); David Couper, Fionbarr Farrell and especially Shirley Duffy (fencing); Leon McSherry and Richie Cullen (Taekwon-Do, Sandymount); Scott Langley (Irishtown Karate Club). I was provided with valuable information about soccer in general by Christopher K. Brennan and about tennis in general by Gail Wolfe.

The part about building the Aviva Stadium would not have been possible without the kind support of Roddy Guiney of Wilson Hartnell and of Sinéad Jackman, who showed me around and was full of information.

Many of the photographs are my own and I thank all the clubs who let me photograph pavilions and pitches. Other photographs were provided by the clubs. I also have to thank Adrian Boehm, Douglas Clark, David Doyle, Shirley Duffy, Maurice Frazer, Philip Murphy, Ken Richardson and Gerard Siggins for letting me use photographs they took or sourced.

There are many more people who supported me with information and by showing their interest in the progress of this book. I am grateful to all of them.

A big thank you has to go to Ronan Colgan and Beth Amphlett of The History Press Ireland who were always friendly, patient and full of good and helpful ideas.

Historical Background

1

This book is concerned with sport and its history in the area that now is known as Dublin 4 and which was formerly Pembroke Township. Even though originally 'sport' meant any diversion or recreation, including hunting, shooting and mind sports, for instance board games like chess and card games like bridge, this book only deals with the exercise of the (human) body.

The first Irish inhabitants of this area were a sept of the Uí Briúin Cualand, known during the Viking times as Mac Gilla Mo Cholmóc and in Norman times as FitzDermot. After the arrival of the Vikings their kings of Dyfflin ruled the area, the last dynasty of which were known under their Irish name MacTurcaill rather than their Viking name Thorkelson. After the coming of the Normans the coastal land south of Dublin was in turns owned by the de Ridelesford, Bagod and FitzWilliam families, with some other families occupying smaller parts. The last major landlords, the Herberts (Earls of Pembroke), are descendants of the Viscounts Fitzwilliam in the female line.

The most common family name of Dublin and the coastal area south of it is Byrne, from the 'Wild Irish' tribe Ó Broin; the second most common name is Doyle from Dubhghall, the dark stranger (i.e. the Danish Viking). This indicates that the majority of the inhabitants of this area have Irish and Viking ancestors. They were country people even though Dublin City had an interest and influence in the area that lay in the 'County of the City of Dublin'. History in general only records the lords of the area. The people who worked the land and minded the animals as well as the craftsmen and -women are rarely mentioned. Until the late nineteenth century those people did not have much leisure for sport.

In 1842 the area of Dublin City was re-defined and reduced in size. The Circular Road became the new city border, circling the area that nowadays is enclosed by the canals. After this re-definition, the area later to become Dublin 4 was in the county of Dublin. Counties were ruled by a grand jury, similar to a county council, except that members were not elected but installed by the high sheriff of the county, who himself was a representative of the Crown. The justices in a grand jury (usually land-owners) set the rates to be paid for any work done by the county. For that reason, rates tended to be set as low as possible and accordingly very little was done. From 1828 onwards, certain areas could, by Act of Parliament, become townships and assume responsibility for such matters as build-ing regulations, lighting, water, sewage, road paving and public health. Through roads and bridges stayed in the hands of the grand jury of the county. In 1863 the south-eastern part of modern Dublin City, more or less the part that now is Dublin 4, became such a township, a town in its own right with the name 'Pembroke Township' (1863–1898) and 'Pembroke Urban District' (1898–1930), taking its name from the Earl of Pembroke, the major landowner in the new township.

Pembroke Township was a mixed community with well-to-do middle-class people especially in the southern part of Donnybrook, Ballsbridge and Sandymount (Ailesbury Road, Pembroke Road, Merrion Road, Park Avenue and Sydney Parade), but it also included the villages of Ringsend and Irishtown, where the inhabitants were by and large working-class and poor. There was no universal franchise at that time. Voters had to be male, of age and possessed of a certain amount of property. In the 1890s, plans to broaden the municipal franchise met with staunch resistance. In February 1892, for instance, the chairman of the Pembroke Town Council complained to the Attorney General that the planned law would establish manhood suffrage in the election of commissioners and as they would also have the right to be elected as commissioners that might lead to the 'curious spectacle of a Board of Commissioners composed of inhabitants of cabins'.[1]

The protest was in vain. The Local Government Act of 1898 extended the franchise for local government, not only giving the vote to all male inhabitants of age, but to all women who were heads of households as well, thus changing the political situation in what from then on was called Pembroke Urban District.

Ringsend, although prosperous in the eighteenth century prior to the con-struction of first Howth and then Kingstown (now Dún Laoghaire) harbours, declined after those ports had been built. Séamas Ó Maitiú describes it in his *Dublin's Suburban Towns 1834–1930* as having had fishing, salt and glass industries in the eighteenth century, but states that in the mid-nineteenth century it had become poor and dilapidated, with both fishing and boat-building greatly reduced.

From the 1890s, the situation improved for Ringsend: the first Pembroke Cottages were built to give improved housing; in 1893 Pembroke Technical and Ringsend Fishery School was inaugurated to provide better education for fishermen and craftsmen; in 1903 the Pembroke Estate offered Herbert Park and in 1905 Ringsend Park to the township, which developed the land, including creating pitches for sport.

Donnybrook is the oldest part of Pembroke Township. It had been a farming community for many centuries and remained so into modern times. Even in the first years of the new Pembroke Township it is reported in 1867 that Donnybrook was 'infested with pigs and stray animals'.[2]

At the beginning of the twentieth century, Pembroke Cottages and St Broc's Cottages were built for the working-class inhabitants of Donnybrook. The cottages on Beaver Row are nearly ninety years older. They were erected around 1815 by the brothers Wright, owners of a beaver hat factory, in an area that later had playing fields for GAA, soccer and rugby.

Donnybrook village included a castle, manor houses and villas. In general, the further south in Pembroke Township its inhabitants lived, the more affluent they were. Ballsbridge and Sandymount had big houses, terraced, semi-detached or detached dwellings, but there were cabins and cottages as well. In this township, middle-class families sent their sons to schools in England, where they played cricket and rugby. Others sent them to Irish schools like Wesley or Bective College or, if they were Catholics, to Belvedere or Blackrock College, all of which are still famous for their rugby teams. In the case of Bective, the rugby club keeps up the name of a school that no longer exists.

Large parts of Pembroke Township, especially in the central and southern part, were developed from the 1860s onwards; houses in Clyde Road for instance were built in 1866 and Ailesbury Road was developed around the same time. At the time sports clubs were founded, the township still had many free spaces which could be and were used for sport pitches. After finishing school either in England or here, young men went on playing the sports they had enjoyed during their school time, first at university and later in the newly established clubs.

Rugby Town?

People might think of this area as Rugby Town, the playground of Ross O'Carroll-Kelly, but the question mark after the title is there for a reason: Many other sports were played in Pembroke Township and are played now in Dublin 4. The area is world-famous as the home of the Irish National Rugby Stadium, but there is much more than that. Soccer, for instance, has more clubs in the area than rugby.

The list of sports, including school sports, played in this area now or in the past is impressive:

Archery	Gaelic Football	Sailing
Badminton	Golf	Soccer
Basketball	Gymnastics	Speedway Racing
Bowls (Lawn)	Hockey	Squash
Boxing	Horse Car Racing	Swimming
Camogie	Horseshoe Pitching	Taekwon-Do
Cycling	Hurling	Table Tennis
Cricket	Karate	Tennis
Croquet	Kick-boxing	Track and Field
Cross-Country Running	Netball	Water Polo
Equestrian	Rounders	Windsurfing
Fencing	Rowing	
Frisbee	Rugby	

Overview of Sport in Dublin 4

Area

The areas of Pembroke Township and Dublin 4 are not exactly the same. Apart from land reclamations after the incorporation of Pembroke Township into the City of Dublin, Pembroke Township included only land of the Barony of Dublin whereas Dublin 4 includes an area that was part of the Barony of Rathdowne. For the modern inhabitants, the borders within the area are in no way fixed. University College Dublin, for instance, gives 'Dublin 4' as the address for the whole Belfield Campus, even though most of it – including its sport complex – is not situated in the area of Dublin City but in the County of Dún Laoghaire-Rathdown. For this reason, UCD sport clubs do not figure in this book. For ease of general use, however, in all other respects the terms Pembroke Township and Dublin 4 will be used interchangeably in this book.

The beginning

Sport activities are recorded in this area before Pembroke Township or Dublin 4 was founded. Surprisingly, one of the earliest records refers to winter sports. Mentioning that a Viking bone skate was found in Dublin, Peter Somerville-Large explains that in earlier centuries the climate had been harsher in this area and that there had been very cold winters, particularly in the years 914, 1000 and 1095. He suggests that skates like the one found in Dublin had perhaps been used 'on the frozen slobland around Ballsbridge'.

It is likely that a thousand years ago the Viking owner of that skate would have used it for fast movement across flooded and then frozen ground, but that while doing so he did not think of anything we would describe as sport.

Cricket was first mentioned in the Dublin area in 1656 when a large number of bats and balls were given up for burning as Cromwell had ordered their destruction.[4] Bowen suggests that cricket is a Celtic game, arguing that the inventors were a group with a measuring system based on the number 11. He found one in the Celtic tribe of the Belgian Atrebates, who lived in what is now French Flanders, where cricket was first mentioned (in 1478), but also in Kent and Sussex, an area that has a high percentage of inhabitants with a particular Celtic blood group and also is the area where cricket first appeared in England.

According to Bowen, the first reported cricket match in Ireland was Dublin Garrison v. All Ireland in 1792 and the first recorded century in Ireland happened in 1800, in a match between the Coldstream Guards and the Third Guards so that the description of cricket as one of the 'garrison sports' seems appropriate. Later though, in the years between 1829 and 1879, Bowen reports the forming of twenty county clubs in Ireland, most if not all of them no longer in existence, at least not in their original form. The (amateur) cricketers of those clubs are referred to as 'Gentlemen', which points to the fact that cricket was a sport for the leisured classes. (Professional cricketers were referred to as 'Players'.)

According to the history of Clanna Gael-Fontenoy GAA Club, Gaelic football was played on Merrion Fields and hurling on Irishtown Green in the eighteenth century. The latter is corroborated by an announcement in September 1757, as quoted by S.J. King:

> ... the *Universal Advertiser* announced a hurling match on Irishtown Green near Dublin between 'Married Men and Bachelors for 50 gns. a side, exactly at 4 o'clock. The Green is to be corded.' Obviously a fine crowd was expected.[5]

More than 100 years later, an important football match took place in Beech Hill: the first All-Ireland football final, which is commemorated on Beech Hill Avenue in Donnybrook.

The idea of a club exclusively for sportspeople was developed in the eighteenth century, at least in the English-speaking world. The Jockey Club is probably the oldest, with a founding date of 1750 or, according to other authors, 1720; Marylebone Cricket Club was founded in 1787; the oldest association football club, Cambridge University AFC, was founded in 1856.

One of the first sport clubs in Ireland was Phoenix Cricket Club, established in 1830. It has a connection with the area covered here, as the club moved from Phoenix Park in 1835, where they had played from 1830 on, to play their matches in open fields south of the canal in an area which was described as 'behind Upper Baggot Street'.[6] This area later became part

FIRST ALL IRELAND
FOOTBALL FINAL
PLAYED AT BEECH HILL
29th APRIL 1888
LIMERICK (Commercials)
v
DUNDALK (Young Irelands)
LIMERICK WINNERS
by 1-4 to 0-3

Plaque on Beech Hill Avenue commemorating the first All-Ireland football final.

of Dublin 4. They played in the Upper Baggot Street area until 1838. The first cricket club with its address in Dublin 4 was founded in 1868, one year before the first rugby club in this area.

Henry W.D. Dunlop.
(Courtesy of Lansdowne FC)

Instilling discipline into the members of a sport club seems to have been difficult, at least in the beginning, as it is reported that 'Punctuality still remains a virtue unknown to football men, and often sorely tries the patience of many an anxious captain'.[7]

Arguably the most important, even if not the oldest, sport club in Dublin 4 from a historian's viewpoint was the Irish Champion Athletic Club. Henry Wallace Doveton Dunlop (1844–1930) had studied engineering in Trinity College Dublin and was a very good sportsman himself. In 1871 he organised the first All-Ireland Athletic Championship in Trinity College and, following that, founded the Royal Irish Athletic Club in May 1872, which in the same year was renamed the Irish Champion Athletic Club. Although he had the approval of the provost of Dublin University, the provost had not consulted the Board, which forbade any further meetings of the Athletic Club on college grounds. One of the reasons was that the Athletic Club included gentlemen who were not members of Trinity.

Dunlop had a grander scale in mind. In December 1872, after initially considering grounds at Serpentine Avenue in Sandymount and Sydney Parade in Merrion, he took a sixty-nine-year lease from the Pembroke Estate for an area of 8.25 acres in the townland of Beggarsbush, now regarded as part of Irishtown, where Beggarsbush townland meets Ballsbridge and Sandymount townlands, at Lansdowne Road between the railway and the Dodder. The rent was £60 per annum. *The Irish Times* published a list of donations for the club in May 1873. This list is topped by the Earl of Pembroke, who donated £25.[8] He was one of the eighteen patrons, of whom Sir Arthur Guinness was another, but only donating £5. Beside the Irish Champion Athletic Club, Dunlop established the Lansdowne Tennis Club, the Lansdowne Archery Club, the Lansdowne Cricket Club, the Lansdowne Croquet Club and, in his own words, '... last but not least the Lansdowne Rugby Football Club – colours, red, black and yellow'.[9] He explains that his reason for establishing the rugby club was that he wanted to keep his athletes active in winter.

In 1904 Dunlop sold the lease to Harry Sheppard, then treasurer of the Irish Rugby Football Union (IRFU). The IRFU had been founded by merging the Irish Football Union and the Northern Union in 1879; the inaugural general meeting was held on 5 February 1880 at 63 Grafton Street, Dublin. Sheppard died in 1906 and the IRFU bought the lease for £200 from his mother. It then built the first covered stand alongside the railway in 1908. More additions and alterations followed and after the latest enormous change, the stadium, now called Aviva Stadium and owned jointly by the IRFU and the Football Association of Ireland (FAI), dominates the skyline of Dublin 4.

The connections between the Dunlop family and Lansdowne Road lasts into this century as two of Dunlop's great-grandsons were the mascots at the first rugby match ever in the new Aviva Stadium.

Sport was not only promoted by clubs; sport was part of many celebrations, especially at the end of the nineteenth century. An example from the Dublin 4 area is an event that took place in May 1892. When the Masonic Female Orphan School's centenary celebration and grand bazaar were held in Ballsbridge, an Ireland v. England tennis championship was held and there were also cycling and athletics events.[10]

Some sport clubs started in firms or organisations, for instance The Railway and Steampacket Companies Irish Athletic and Social Union, which held its first general meeting in June 1904. Their purpose was 'to promote and encourage sport and games and other forms of social and athletic activities among the staffs of the Railway and Steampacket Companies represented in Ireland, the Irish Railway Clearing House (IRCH), the Dublin United Tramway Co. and the Grand Canal Company'.[11] Irish Railway Clearing House is credited with the idea of founding this union of clubs as they had had soccer and cricket clubs in the 1903 season already.

In later years, they shortened the 'unmanageable' title of the club(s) to 'Railway Union' and club members usually refer to it just as 'Railway'. In 1943 they took a fifty-year lease on the ground from the Pembroke Estate and finally bought out the freehold in 1987 for £42,000.

Imported versus Indigenous Ball Sports

The founders and first councillors of Pembroke Township were middle-class, Protestant and Unionist and looked east to Britain for their roots, so it is not surprising that we find a strong British influence in the sports played in Dublin 4.

Rugby

Table 1: City and Co. Dublin rugby clubs founded before 1931

Name	Address	Founded
Dublin University FC	College Park	1854
Wanderers FC	Ballsbridge / Irishtown	1869
Lansdowne FC	Irishtown	1872
Clontarf RFC	Clontarf	1876
Bective Rangers FC	Donnybrook	1881
Blackrock College RFC	Blackrock	1882
Monkstown FC	Sandymount	1883
Old Wesley RFC	Donnybrook	1891
RCSI	Santry	1896
DLSP FC	Kilternan	1899
St Mary's College RFC	Templeogue	1900

Railway Union RFC	*Sandymount*	*1904*
Parkmore RFC	Terenure College	1907
UCD RFC	Belfield	1910
Malahide RFC	Malahide	1922
CYM-Terenure Rugby	Terenure	1924
Suttonians RFC	Sutton	1924
Balbriggan RFC	Balbriggan	1925
Skerries RFC	Skerries	1926
Old Belvedere RFC	*Donnybrook*	*1930*

Table 1 shows twenty rugby clubs which were founded in the city and county of Dublin between 1854 and 1930 and still exist. Seven of them, shown in italics in Table 1, are situated in Dublin 4. This is an impressive 35 per cent. All seven are in the southern half of Dublin 4 in the Ballsbridge/Donnybrook/Sandymount area.

Cricket

Table 2: City and Co. Dublin cricket clubs founded before 1931

Name	Address	Founded
Phoenix CC	Phoenix Park	1830
Dublin University CC	TCD	1835
Leinster CC	Rathmines	1852
Malahide CC	Malahide	1861
Civil Service CC	Phoenix Park	1863
Pembroke CC	*Sandymount*	*1868*
Clontarf CC	Clontarf	1876
YMCA CC	*Sandymount*	*1890*
Merrion CC	*Donnybrook*	*1892*
Railway Union CC	*Sandymount*	*1904*
CYM Terenure CC	Terenure	1904

The distribution of cricket clubs is similar to that of rugby clubs. Four of the extant cricket clubs in the city and county of Dublin that were founded before

1930 are in Dublin 4, a third of all cricket clubs in the city and county at that time. Table 2 shows the cricket clubs in Dublin 4 in italics. They had professionals from early on: in the 1911 census for Sandymount, two gentlemen gave their occupation as 'professional cricketer', one of whom lived on-site, in a three-room lodge on the Pembroke CC Grounds.

Hockey

In 1930, when Pembroke was incorporated into Dublin City, ten hockey clubs existed in the city and county of Dublin. Table 3 shows those hockey clubs, again with the five in Dublin 4 in italics. Three Rock Rovers Hockey Club is included in those because they played in Londonbridge Avenue, Irishtown, before they moved to Rathfarnham in 1981.

Table 3: City and Co. Dublin Hockey Clubs founded until 1931

Name	Address	Founded	Members
Avoca	Blackrock	1891	men & women
Dublin University	Santry	1893	men & women
Three Rock Rovers	Rathfarnham	1893	men & women
Monkstown	Monkstown	1894	men & women
Railway Union	Sandymount	1904	men & women
YMCA	Sandymount	1908	men & women
Muckross	Donnybrook	1918	women only
Pembroke Wanderers	Ballsbridge	1922	men & women
Loreto	Rathfarnham	1926	women only
St James's Gate	Crumlin Road	1928	men & women

GAA

Michael Cusack, who was a good athlete, taught at several schools, including Blackrock College and Clongowes Wood. Later he had his own academy in which he prepared young men for the civil service. In 1879 he started a rugby club for students of his academy. Apart from playing himself in this club, he also acted as honorary secretary and honorary treasurer. He dropped rugby in 1883 and changed the academy sport to hurling.[12]

In 1884 Cusack founded the Gaelic Athletic Association together with Maurice Davin. In March 1901, he lived in Beach Road, Sandymount.[13] The GAA originally catered for athletics as well as traditional team sports but gave up control of athletics in 1922.[14] Their website now lists as 'Our Games' football, hurling, ladies football, camogie, handball and rounders, although handball and rounders feature less often in the programmes of their clubs. Hurling is by far the oldest of the sports. Mythological references trace it back to the second millennium BCE, which would make it a sport played in Ireland before the arrival of the Celts.

In the years following the founding of the GAA, several clubs were formed in Dublin 4. Over time they merged into Clanna Gael-Fontenoy, which is the sole GAA club in the area today.

Table 4 shows the GAA clubs that merged into Clanna Gael-Fontenoy. It also shows that the earliest GAA club in this area was founded in 1886, only two years after the founding of the GAA.

Table 4: GAA clubs in Dublin 4

Name	Original Address	Founded
Ed Grays	Merrion	1886
Fontenoy	Bath Avenue	17/10/1887
Brothers Sheares	Baggot Street	1887
H.J. McCracken's	Ballsbridge	1887
Shamrock GFC	Fenian Street / Ringsend	1887
Isles of the Sea	Ringsend	before 1890
Michael Dwyer	Ringsend	1891
Hillside GFC	Westland Row	1893
Erin's Isle GFC	Ringsend	early 1900s
Sandymount GFC	Sandymount	1903
St Andrew's	Pearse Street / Ringsend	1906
St Mary's	Donnybrook	1909
Donnybrook Davitts	Donnybrook	1916 & c. 2000
Inishfaels	Leeson Street / Pembroke Street	early twentieth century
Peadar Macken's	Pearse Street / Ringsend	1917
Kevin Barry GFC	Haddington Road	1921
Desmond GFC	Donnybrook	early 1920s
Clanna Gael	Drumcondra / Ringsend	1929

Soccer

While it might be tempting to conclude that the northern half of Dublin 4 was nationalist and played GAA whereas the southern half was Unionist and therefore preferred imported sports, this would be ignoring another important sport: association football or soccer.

Like Gaelic football, soccer was played mainly by the working class. Sports like rugby, cricket and hockey were played by boys and young men of the middle class who attended fee-paying secondary schools. Working-class families did not have the money to pay school fees and also needed the earning power of their children much earlier than more affluent families. The 1901 census shows that some young people living in the poorer areas of Dublin 4 were working at the age of 13 or 14.

In the context of GAA and soccer, it is important to remember rule 27 of the GAA, 'The Ban'. In place from 1904 to 1971, this rule forbade GAA members to practise and even to watch 'garrison sports'. Gaelic football and even hurling players did not really have qualms about playing soccer; there are mentions in match descriptions of a Gaelic player that had been caught by an official (or an informer) doing so. According to rule 27, such a player would be expelled from the GAA. Nonetheless these instances did occur. Not all GAA members approved of the rule, as the following letter shows:

Fontenoy Hurling Club
To the Editor of Freeman's Journal

Dear Sir – A member of our minor team viz. George Kenna, age 17 years and one month, was objected to by one of the Fianna Oga na hEireann as an illegal player in the minor contest of the Hurling League. They state he played 'Soccer' on the 11th April, present year, and we lost the points on this ground. Now I would like to know can it be possible that such a rule does exist that a youth of his age is debarred from participating in any of the competitions under GAA rules for life? If such a rule does exist permit me to point out to the governing body of the GAA that it is a monstrous one, and one that will not encourage the youth to play or foster our manly pastimes. Up to six months ago a youth of his age had no other game only that of the alien, and now youths who always played 'Soccer', because they had no other game to play, and are now playing

Gaelic, are singled out by clubs who are not their equal in the field getting points deducted off them. For what? I could well understand such a rule applying to senior football, which rule, I believe, was carried to cope with same. But surely, in all common sense, outside anything else, there is no such rule applicable to minor hurling teams. If there is it is stretching the thing a bit too far, and the sooner abolished the better. – Yours faithfully

James Mullany,
48, Tritonville Road, Sandymount
28th October, 1903.[15]

James Joseph Mullany seems to have been the first honorary secretary of Fontenoy Hurling Club, as, according to the Dublin County Board minutes of 1901, Mr James Mullany, of 4 Rosemount Terrace, Londonbridge Road, Sandymount, affiliated Fontenoy as a Hurling Club.[16] According to the 1901 and 1911 censuses, he was 26 years old when he wrote the above letter, the eldest of twelve children of an ironmonger's assistant. In 1901 he was a timber salesman and in 1911 a commercial traveller, arguably a typical committee member of a GAA club at that time.

In the area of Dublin 4, soccer seems to have become organised later than the Gaelic sports. The oldest soccer club in this area is younger than five of the GAA clubs shown in Table 4.

Table 5: Extant soccer clubs founded in Dublin 4

Name	Area	Founded	Pitch (today)
Liffey Wanderers FC	Ringsend	1883	Irishtown Stadium
Shelbourne FC	Irishtown	1895	Tolka Park
Shamrock Rovers FC	Ringsend	1901	Tallaght
Railway Union FC	Sandymount	1904	Sandymount
St Mark's Athletic FC	Ringsend	1906	Ringsend Park

Football is a very old team sport, frequently forbidden during the Middle Ages as it was supposed to cause the players to neglect their archery practice. Apart from that, there were no approved rules and for centuries the rules of the game differed from area to area or even from village to village. It was only during the mid-nineteenth century that different set of rules started to appear for the four versions of football now known as Gaelic football, soccer, rugby and American football. Even at times when the separation of those four types of football should have been quite clear and accepted, there were matches that showed their near relationship, as an article in the *Freeman's Journal* in 1879 shows. This article describes a match which was neither played according to the association football nor the rugby football rules as running with the ball was strictly prohibited. On the other hand, a 'total absence of offside' seems to have destroyed the sense of a team as the reporter describes its character as a match during which every man played for himself. For some unexplained reason, the number of players was different in the teams also, with ten players in the team of the past pupils and fifteen in the team of present pupils. It is reported that some very good dribbling was shown on both sides, but with the unequal size of the teams it was no surprise that the present pupils won, partly because they could afford to have some players 'loitering' near the posts to await balls that the field players of their team passed to them. Despite not being in school anymore but in office, at least some of the past pupils were quite energetic, as was reported about a then well-known solicitor in Dublin who 'covered himself with glory in pursuit of which he got equally covered with mud'.[17]

Tennis

Lawn tennis replaced croquet as a fashionable sport for ladies in the second half of the nineteenth century.

Table 6: Tennis clubs in Dublin 4

Name	Address	Courts	Surface	Founded
Lansdowne LTC	Irishtown	11	Artificial grass	1875
Donnybrook LTC	Donnybrook	8	Artificial grass	1893
Claremont Railway Union LTC	Sandymount	10	Artificial grass	1904/08
Bective LTC	Donnybrook	7	Artificial grass	1921
Elm Park (Tennis Club)	Donnybrook	7+7	All weather + grass	1926

The two years given for Claremont Railway Union refer to the years the two clubs were founded. They merged in 1982.

Sport events were not only organised by clubs; schools also had a great influence. A report on the centenary bazaar for the Masonic Female Orphan

School in 1892 remarks that on Friday 20 May, the RDS jumping grounds were, among other events, the scene of the first ever international lawn tennis contest between Ireland and England. This international competition was intended as a warm-up to 'Fitzwilliam Week', as the Irish Championship was known then.[18]

That success in sport did not always come via a club is shown by the case of John Pius Boland, the second son of the baker and mill owner Patrick Boland. John Pius was regarded as a very good athlete with an especially good ability for tennis. J.P. Boland, then 26 years of age, was studying in Bonn in 1896 when he decided to travel to Athens to see the classical sites but also to look at the first modern Olympic Games. While in Athens, he visited a friend, Thrasyvoulos Manos, who happened to be a member of the organising committee. Boland had had no thought of participating in the Games, but Manos entered him in the tennis tournament. Boland went on to win the singles tournament, beating Friedrich Traun of Germany in the final. He then won the double event as well, partnered with Traun.

There is a story that when the Union flag and the German flag were run up the flagpole to honour their victory, Boland pointed out to the man hoisting the flags that he was Irish, adding 'It [the Irish flag]'s a gold harp on a green ground, we hope'. The officials agreed to have an Irish flag prepared.[19]

The story about the flag is dubious, however, as according to other sources J.P. Boland had described himself as English until he read in *Oxford Magazine* that his tennis victories were ascribed to England.[20]

J.P. Boland was born in Capel Street, but as Boland's Flour Mills, the largest part of his family's firm, was situated on the Ringsend side of the Grand Canal Basin it is appropriate to mention him here. He was after all the first Irish gold medallist at Olympic Games.

Golf

It is often said that behind the foundation of almost every golf club in the world you will find a native Scot, or at least somebody of Scottish extraction.[21] As far as Ireland is concerned, that might be true. Golf was introduced into Ireland by officers of various Scottish regiments stationed here, notably the Black Watch (Am Freiceadan Dubh, or 42nd Regiment of Foot). Dublin 4 only ever had one golf course: Elm Park.

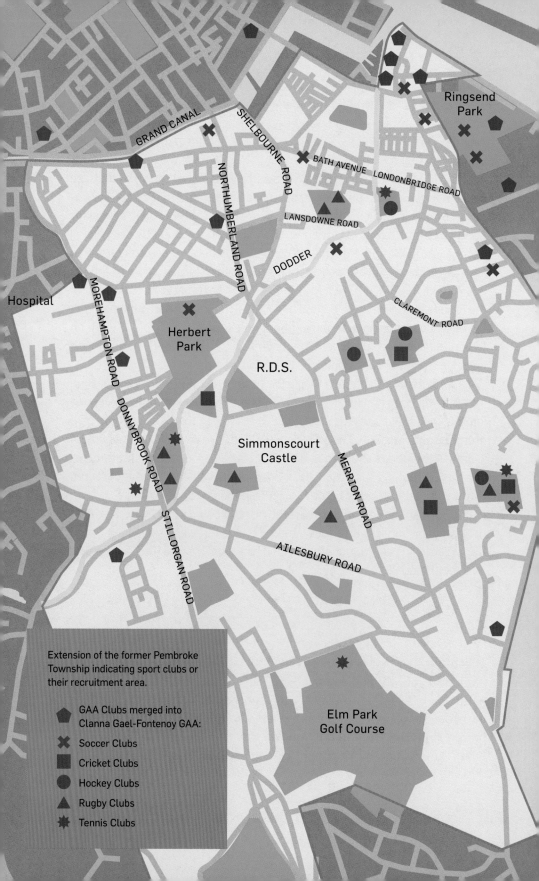

GRAND CANAL

SHELBOURNE ROAD

BATH AVENUE

LONDONBRIDGE ROAD

Ringsend Park

NORTHUMBERLAND ROAD

LANSDOWNE ROAD

DODDER

Hospital

CLAREMONT ROAD

MOREHAMPTON ROAD

Herbert Park

R.D.S.

DONNYBROOK ROAD

Simmonscourt Castle

MERRION ROAD

STILLORGAN ROAD

AILESBURY ROAD

Elm Park Golf Course

Extension of the former Pembroke Township indicating sport clubs or their recruitment area.

GAA Clubs merged into Clanna Gael-Fontenoy GAA:

Soccer Clubs

Cricket Clubs

Hockey Clubs

Rugby Clubs

Tennis Clubs

Location of Imported and Indigenous Sports in D4

The map shows playing fields for rugby, cricket, hockey, tennis, soccer and GAA or – in the case of the two latter sports – the area in which the clubs recruited their players. It can be seen that sports preferred by the working classes – Gaelic sports and soccer – are concentrated in the northern and north-western part of the surveyed area. Sports played by the middle classes – rugby, cricket, hockey and tennis – are concentrated further south and south-east.

The map does not show venues for lawn bowls (Railway Union and Herbert Park), horse jumping (RDS), track and field or karate (both Irishtown Stadium), rowing (Ringsend), swimming (South Wall and the EBS Sports Centre (Sportsco), Ringsend) or venues for sports that have disappeared from this area, like cycle races, bicycle polo and boxing.

The blue lines on the map show the borders of former Pembroke Township, which did not include the direct neighbourhood of the Grand Canal Docks.

It is interesting to check the mobility of players in different sports. Quite often to this day local rugby clubs attract players from outside the area; during the last years, for instance, Lansdowne FC had Felipe Contepomi from the Argentine, Shane Horgan from County Meath, Gordon D'Arcy from County Wexford and Dave Kearney from County Louth. Soccer clubs of the area, on the other hand, often export players. Ringsend and Irishtown soccer players have strong connections with Liverpool and Manchester clubs but can be found in other English and Scottish clubs as well.

Lawn Bowls

In around 1670, Eleanor Fitzwilliam, Countess of Tyrconnell, of Merrion Castle was addressed by the then Lord Lieutenant, the Duke of Ormonde, to ask her for sods as the mayor and sheriffs of Dublin Corporation planned to make a bowling green on Oxmantown Green. They had informed the Lord Lieutenant that neither sods dug up from Oxmantown or even St Stephen's Green were suitable, but that they had heard that suitable sods for a bowling green could be found in Merrion. Consequently, the duke asked the countess politely to let Dublin Corporation have the necessary sods to be removed from 'where they may be best spared'.[22]

This was probably the earliest mention of bowling in what later became Dublin 4. Now the oldest bowling green still in use in Dublin is the one of Railway Union. Decades later a second bowling green in Dublin 4 was laid out in Herbert Park.

Other Sports

As far as equestrian sports are concerned, the RDS comes to mind immediately with its Spring Shows and Horse Shows, which have included jumping contests since 1868. In the beginning, these shows took place on Leinster Lawn, but since 1881 they have been held in Ballsbridge. Cycling races and bicycle polo were well known in cycling clubs in Dublin 4 in the last decades of the nineteenth century. Athletics in the sense of field and track sport has been one of the reasons H.W.D. Dunlop built his 'Royal Irish Park Stadium' in Lansdowne Road. The RDS as well as the Lansdowne Road Stadium were hosts for both cycling and athletic events. There are reports of a boxing club in the area as well but neither its foundation date nor its location could be ascertained. Martial arts were introduced in the area in the early 1990s.

Kayaking class in Grand Canal Basin.

As far as water sports are concerned, the Half Moon Swimming Club, founded in 1898, still provides possibilities for swimming in the sea. In the eighteenth and nineteenth centuries, there were different bathing places along the coast from the Merrion Gates to Irishtown and Ringsend, but they catered more for leisure than for sport; sea-bathing was all the fashion in the eighteenth, nineteenth and early twentieth centuries. The Dublin & Kingstown Railway Company owned some baths on the coast along its line.[23] Before the baths on Merrion Strand were built, the 1865 OS map shows 'Merrion Baths' more or less at Merrion Gates and 'bathing pools' in the Ringsend area, where Ringsend Park is now. Ringsend boasted many rowing clubs during the time of Pembroke Township but all rowing clubs from this time either folded or moved up the Liffey to Islandbridge. What remained are the two East Coast rowing clubs in Ringsend, which were founded after Pembroke Urban District had been incorporated into Dublin Corporation.

During the last years, water sports have taken advantage of the possibilities of the Grand Canal Basin. Schools for wakeboarding and kayaking have been established there in recent years and their practice and/or competitions can be watched from time to time, sometimes even from Grand Canal Dock DART Station.

For a short time during the first years of the twenty-first century, Ballsbridge had a spot for a sport that rarely makes headlines: horseshoe pitching. Some mementoes still exist.

The **Ballsbridge Horseshoe Pitching Club** was founded in 1992. In 2001 they were granted £100,000 by the Department of Sport to transform the former public convenience at Anglesea Road near Ball's Bridge into a two-storey clubhouse and were given the triangular site between Anglesea Road, the Dodder and the bridge by Dublin City Council in 2002 as their pitch. After opposition, first against the grant and then against the plans for the clubhouse, they lost the subsidy. Ballsbridge Horseshoe Pitchers Club Ltd was dissolved as a company on 5 August 2007. The public convenience was demolished in August 2014 and the site will be used to allow for extensive flood-relief work. A small plaque and a horseshoe nailed to one of the trees facing Merrion Road keeps the memory of the club alive.

Sign of Ballsbridge Park Horseshoe Pitchers Club.

School Sports

4

Schools help children to develop their physical and social abilities by teaching different sports from a very young age.

Primary Schools

Dublin 4 has over a dozen primary schools, including schools for pupils with special needs. Six of the general primary schools are situated in Ballsbridge, two are in Donnybrook, one in Irishtown, two in Ringsend and two in Sandymount. St Conleth's and St Michael's in Ballsbridge, both connected to secondary schools, stress their involvement in rugby, though St Michael's also highlights GAA and basketball among the many sports they offer. The two Sandymount schools Scoil Mhuire (Lakelands) for girls and Star of the Sea for boys are very successful in GAA. In 2014, for instance, the girls of Scoil Mhuire won the Corn Comhar Linn in the Cumann na mBunscol Áth Cliath final and the boys of the Star of the Sea won the Corn Mhic Chaoilte.

Secondary Schools

Of the seven secondary schools existing in this area, two are in Ballsbridge, three in Donnybrook and one each in Ringsend and in Sandymount. They all have physical education (PE) in their curriculum, but they also offer extra-curricular sports education.

St Conleth's College stresses that it is a traditional rugby school but they also offer tennis, squash and basketball and are quite well known for their fencing team.

St Michael's College is very well known for its rugby teams, which in 2012 won both the senior and the junior Leinster school rugby cup. They offer GAA and basketball as well and have a cycling club, a cross-country team, tennis squads, self-defence/kick-boxing and archery.

Muckross Park College is known for hockey, but they also have teams for basketball, cricket, an equestrian team and squads for tennis and swimming. They have a strong athletic tradition and compete in the National Schools' Cross-Country Championship and the National Schools' Track and Field Competition.

John Scottus School provides twice the amount of time for physical education than the Department of Education has set as the minimum. They offer basketball as well as soccer for boys and hockey for girls as extra-curricular activities.

The Teresian School is situated in the grounds of the former Donnybrook Cottage in the townland Roebuck, an area that did not belong to Pembroke Township, but now is part of Donnybrook and Dublin 4. They have teams for hockey and basketball.

Ringsend College started a new initiative in 2014 offering GAA sports scholarships to new pupils. The programme enables students to be coached in football, hurling and camogie for boys and girls. They not only receive training but also classes on tactics, team play, nutrition and diet.

Marian College provides as extra-curricular sports rugby, soccer, GAA, basketball, athletics and cricket beside the rarely offered table tennis. They regard rugby as their main sport. Singular for a school in this area, they have a water polo team and water polo is the sport they are best known for.

Another school should be mentioned as it had a long history, but does not exist anymore today: The **Masonic Female Orphan School** (1792–1972), was situated from 1852 to 1882 in Burlington House, from 1882 to 1972 in the iconic building that until May 2015 was known as Bewley's Hotel and is now known as Clayton Hotel. It had teams for netball, badminton, tennis, rounders, gymnastics, athletics, cricket and hockey. The school was well known for their hockey teams, their 1st XI winning the Senior Hockey Cup in 1945, 1952 and 1953.[24]

Rugby, Cricket and Hockey

Rugby

One of a rugby club historian's main difficulty might well be in compiling a comprehensive list of pitches on which a club played as in some cases these changed more than once in the early years. This is something rugby clubs have in common with soccer clubs. The reason in both cases is that in the formative years the clubs did not yet have enough funds to lease or even buy a pitch. The exception is Lansdowne FC, which came into being after grounds were leased by Henry Wallace Doveton Dunlop.

Wanderers FC is the oldest rugby club in the area and the second oldest in Ireland after the rugby club of Dublin University. Wanderers were founded in the 1869/70 season before the foundation of the Irish Rugby Football Union IRFU in 1879, so they proudly use 'FC' instead of RFC which is more common among the younger clubs. Most of the founding members seem to have been students of Trinity College Dublin who wanted a second club so that the University Football Club would have an adversary. Membership in the different clubs during the early times seems to have been fluid and multiple memberships were rather common.

The founding of a club was one matter, but the task of finding regular players was another, and far more difficult. Naturally enough many of the leading Trinity players joined immediately, for they were keen to get as many matches as possible, and so much was that the case that when

Lansdowne arrived to join the little circle in 1872 there were several instances of players becoming members of all three clubs.[25]

A photograph of a team in the 1877/8 season shows the players wearing a variety of jerseys and socks.

According to their centenary publication, their first clubhouse was a mud cabin probably at Morehampton Road, 'but later on they moved down to a stable at the rear of the houses on Clyde Road' where Clare Lane or a part of Herbert Park is now.[26] During that stage, they played in a field at Wellington Place, which at that time only had a rather small terrace of houses on its north side.

In January 1880, Wanderers FC had to leave Clyde Road because the field was required for tillage.[27] They leased a pitch in Dunlop's Lansdowne Road ground and have been tenants there ever since. They still have tenant rights in the new Aviva Stadium Complex though the old pavilion is gone. It was tucked into the corner between Lansdowne Road and the railway and looked like a neat cottage from the front, though it was not really that small.

A Wanderers FC team of the 1877/8 season. From left to right, back row: F. Smyley, F. Allen, Wallace Beatty, H. Cox, P. Casement, F.R. Todd, ? Ross. Middle row: A. Darley, F. Harrison, ? Walsh, J.H. Ross-Todd (c), R.M. Peter, T. Spunner, H. Adams. Front row: A.Barlow, H.L. Robinson, A. P. Cronyn. (Courtesy of Wanderers FC)

Old pavilion of Wanderers FC in Lansdowne Road.

A distinguished early member of Wanderers was Frederick W. Moore (1857–1950). He was a horticulturist and became curator of the Trinity College Botanic Garden in Lansdowne Road at the age of 21. Three years later, he followed his father as 'Keeper' (nowadays he would be called 'Director') of the Royal Botanical Garden in Glasnevin, an office that he kept for forty-three years. He was a member of Wanderers for seventy-one years and played until he was 44 years old. During his time as a member, he was four times capped for Ireland. In 1889/1890 he was president of the IRFU and in 1891 president of Wanderers FC. He was knighted in 1911.

Wanderers now have a modern clubhouse as part of the newly developed rugby complex on Lansdowne Road, sharing a building with the IRFU and next to Lansdowne FC.

For many years after 1893, their clubhouse was in 25 South Frederick Street, which their presi-

Sir Frederick W. Moore.
(Courtesy of Wanderers FC)

dent Robert McNevin-Bradshaw had gifted them under a 999-year lease. This clubhouse was important as it provided the bar facilities missing in Lansdowne Road.

Wanderers FC clubhouse, Merrion Road.

Since the 1930s, they also have grounds off the Merrion Road complete with a clubhouse. On a map or in an aerial view, the shape of these grounds is like a child's drawing of a Christmas tree. This shape lets them have two playing fields that are laid out in a 45° angle to each other. Those pitches are mostly used for their junior teams.

They play in jerseys with black-blue-white hoops and blue shorts with over-35, senior, under-20, youths and minis teams.

Lansdowne FC, the second oldest rugby club in the area and third oldest in Ireland, was founded in 1872 by Henry Wallace Doveton Dunlop in Lansdowne Road. The club colours are red, yellow and black according to their letterheads, but red, black and yellow according to the memoirs of H.W.D. Dunlop. Some photographs show the first-mentioned sequence, others the second. The newest photographs on their website show the sequence red, yellow and black. Their shorts are navy. They currently have over-35, senior, under-21, youths and minis teams.

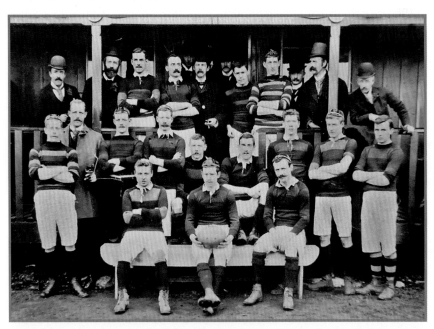

Lansdowne FC, 1st XV, 1893/4. From left to right, back row: J. Anderson, J. Sibthorpe (Hon. Treasurer), G.P. Moyles, A.E. Simson, J.B. Moore, W. Street, E.P. Roe, R.G. Warren, A.K. Toomey, H.W. Dunlop (President). Middle row: J.S. Jameson, R. Dyas, W. Norwood, R. Glass, E.G. Brunker (Hon. Secretary), H. Lesmond, S.C. Smith, G.K. Jouce, F.E. Davies (c). Front row: G. Martin, A.A. Brunker, H.P. Thompson. (Courtesy of Lansdowne FC)

Earlier pavilions on Lansdowne Road have disappeared. H.W.D. Dunlop mentions in his memoirs in the 1920s that the then pavilion was the fourth and that he hoped soon to have something better. When seen from the north across the back pitch, today the two oldest rugby clubs in this area are directly side by side, Wanderers in the taller wing of the building on the right, Lansdowne in the longer and lower wing on the left.

Even before living in the same building on Lansdowne Road, one might have wondered what it felt like for a club to have a competing club at the other end of the pitch. Perhaps the following quotation from Lansdowne member Garry Redmond answers the question:

> Lansdowne and Wanderers have improved on My Dear Old Dutch: we've been together on The Road now for eighty-nine years, which is fair to middling hurling by any standard. Each is to the other, as it were, a sort of covenant running with the land: not much to be done about it except live with it. You get used to anything, they say; though it can sometimes be a hard old station. Probably what takes the harm out of it is that we know that they know that we know – and that we both really care.
>
> As Cork is to Dublin men, so Wanderers to Lansdowne: not so much a club as an attitude of mind. No question of joining them – you beat them, if and when you can.[28]

There are all sorts of stories, old and new, about antagonism between Wanderers and Lansdowne, and in the same article Garry Redmond continues:

> Some of us modern young sirs would wonder at this Draconian non-fraternization. In time we learned how scandalised some of the older Lansdownes had been some years before by the fact that a whole Lansdowne team, having beaten Wanderers in the Cup, had gone off to have a meal and a few jars with them in Jury's afterwards. That sort of thing wasn't done – questions were even asked in Committee.

Lansdowne was and is not only known for the quality of their players, but also for their referees. *The Leinster Rugby Centenary Book* mentions four referees from Lansdowne FC by name: R.W. Jeffares, Ham Lambert, Bobby Mitchell and Kevin Kelleher. Mitchell is praised for his ability to read a game and to control the players so that dirty play or fisticuffs simply did not occur. Kelleher is regarded as the best, not just in Leinster or even in Ireland but anywhere and at any time, which is praise indeed. He was obviously able to see things that a video replay is asked for nowadays before a decision is made. It seems that sometimes players tried to intimidate the referee as the report mentions that no intimidation would stir his decision. It is quite clear that he was regarded as the ideal referee for all times.[29]

Dick Spring, former leader of the Labour Party and Tánaiste, played for Lansdowne FC. The club supplied and still supplies many players for the national team; in 2014, for instance, they had eight 'internationals': Gordon D'Arcy, Dave Kearney, Mike McCarthy, Jordi Murphy, Marty Moore, Eoin Reddan, Dominic Ryan and Devin Toner.

Morehampton FC seems to have come into and gone out of existence in a very short time. Richard M. Peter states in his book *The Origins and Development of Football in Ireland* that the club was formed in 1878 and played on grounds adjoining the Royal Hospital Donnybrook, but that they had to give up the grounds during drainage works and that during that time the members had joined other clubs.[30] The grounds mentioned, between the Royal Hospital and Bloomfield House, were used at the same time by the rugby club of Wesley College and later also by Old Wesley RFC until the Royal Hospital needed it for their own use early in 1906. Today it is used for sport again. Beechwood FC, a schoolboy soccer club, plays some of its matches there.

Bective Rangers FC, next in age among rugby clubs in this area, distinguishes between 'school rugby' and 'club rugby' in its history. The school club was originally called Bective College (past and present pupils) and then, from the 1870s, Bective FC. R.M. Peters includes Bective College in his 'List of Football Clubs, with Names and Addresses of Hon. Secretaries' with their honorary secretary's address as 15 Rutland Square, East, the address of Bective House Seminary for Young Gentlemen (established 1834), though the club does not appear in the sections 'Irish Rugby Football Clubs, with Names of Officers and Reports of the Past Season' or 'Diary of Matches Played During the Past Season'.[31] As Bective Rangers FC, they were founded in 1881. After the closure of the college in 1885, the rugby club was opened to others. The club first trained and played its matches in the Phoenix Park and over subsequent years moved around Dublin, using pitches at Sydney Parade and Ranelagh (Rugby Road). The club played matches at the RDS during the 1890s and 1900s before settling at Donnybrook in around 1910.[32] They have over-35s, senior, junior and minis teams.

Bective Rangers
clubhouse at
Donnybrook Rugby
Grounds.

John Hamilton O'Conor,
Bective Rangers
and Ireland, 1894.
(Courtesy of Gerard Siggins)

They were very strong in the last years of the nineteenth century, with up to three players in the Irish national team. One of those, John Hamilton O'Conor, was at that time the heaviest man in the team, with a weight of 13 stone. Of the fifteen international players that ran out to win against South Africa on 11 June 2016 the lightest was Paddy Jackson at 13 stone 9 pounds. In this team John O'Conor would have been the lightest. He was highly regarded in rugby circles in his time and became president of the IRFU for the 1911/12 season.

One of the club's founders, Harvey du Cros, showed that in his time many sportsmen were all-round sportsmen. Apart from playing rugby, Harvey was an Irish boxing and fencing champion and promoted cycle racing in Dublin, especially in Phoenix Park. Outside sports he was an industrialist: together with John Boyd Dunlop he ran the well-known pneumatic tyre company. He was also involved in the motor car business, a Justice of the Peace and for two years Member of Parliament for Hastings in East Sussex.

Monkstown FC, which was founded in 1883, comes next in the timeline of foundation of rugby clubs in the Pembroke/Dublin 4 area. This club started, as the name suggests, in Monkstown, County Dublin, but in 1901 it moved to the grounds near Sydney Parade in Sandymount, leasing them from

Pitch of Monkstown FC and Pembroke CC.

the Pembroke Estate in the beginning. They share the ground with the Pembroke Cricket Club; the rugby club in residence in winter and the cricket club in summer. In 1983 the two clubs bought the ground and now are co-owners of the site.

One of their members, James Cecil Parke, was capped twenty times for Ireland. Apart from that, he won the mixed double at Wimbledon in 1914 (with Ethel Thomson Larcombe of the UK), which makes him one of two Irish rugby internationals that have won Wimbledon (the other one is Frank Stoker of Lansdowne LTC).

Monkstown FC always had good connections to the military, first to the British Army and after Irish Independence to the Defence Forces. The biennial match between the Irish Defence Forces team and the French Defence Forces team has been played regularly on their grounds.

Monkstown FC play in jerseys with blue and yellow hoops and white shorts. Their teams range from Veterans (Vets) via Seniors and a very active youth section to Minis.

There seems to have been an older club in Monkstown, County Dublin as a report of 1880 hopes that it will be possible to revive this club with 'some of the first rate players who reside in Monkstown'.[33] It is not clear what connection, if any, there is between this older club and the present club.

Monkstown FC 1884/5 season. The gentlemen in suits and bowler hat are: left: H.W. Jones (Hon. Sec.), right: E.F. Russell. The players, from left to right, back row: M.J. Carpendale, T.F. Walters, C.A. D'Alton, R.J. Davenish, A.E. Littlewed, J. Annesley, J.J. Walters. Front row: J.J. McCarthy, D.W. Rambout, W.J.B. McBlain, P.E.S. Reeves (Capt.) (with ball), L.W. Moyes, W.J. Nickson, J.R. Blacker, J. Fitzgerald. (Courtesy of Monkstown FC)

Old Wesley RFC was founded in 1891. From the beginning, it was an open club, a separate club from the college club, but keeping the connection with Wesley College. For the first thirty years, the principal of Wesley College was president of Old Wesley RFC.

There was an older club which, as in the case of Bective, was a school club as distinguished from a 'rugby club', even though, according to R.M. Peter the school club played against non-school rugby clubs for the 1879/80 season. This was the Wesley College Football Club which played, for instance, against the 1st XV of Lansdowne FC.[34] Its captain, Louis McIntosh, was the son of the first headmaster of Wesley College (Maxwell McIntosh, LL.D. (TCD)). In 1887 this school club became a founder member of the Leinster Schools Cup.

The football rules of Wesleyan Connexional School, forerunner of Wesley College, were reported in its school magazine *Eaglet* of 17 May 1862 and quoted in their illustrated history for their 150th anniversary.[35] The same source says that by 1883 matches were internal between two teams of the same school. It also reports that initially past pupils and masters, as well as present pupils, played on the Wesley College teams even after 1891 when Old Wesley Rugby Football Club had been founded, which from the beginning accepted members that had not been pupils of Wesley College. Old Wesley RFC played senior games from 1895. The fact that in the beginning they shared the same grounds with the school club does not make research easy for a historian. Those grounds were in Donnybrook; however, they were not in Donnybrook Stadium, now often described as 'Wesley', but at Bloomfield, on grounds which they had leased from the Royal Hospital. They had to leave those grounds by the end of the 1905/06 season and first moved to Cowper Gardens, Rathmines, and then to Westfield Park, Harold's Cross, which they gave up early in the First World War.

At the turn from the nineteenth to the twentieth century, one of the members of Old Wesley RFC was James Beckett, scion of a well-known family of builders. This James Beckett was a remarkable person. He is described as an extremely versatile player, proficient at scrum-half, outside-half, centre and wing. He did not only play rugby, including for the Leinster provincial team, but was also a good swimmer, winning swimming titles for 100, 220, 440 and 880 yards, some of those more than once. He captained the Irish water polo team many times and was also an Irish high-diving champion. He was a good golfer, a renowned singer and, according to reports, a good cartoonist. He achieved all that while studying medicine.[36] During his later

Old Wesley RFC clubhouse.

Old Wesley RFC *v.* CIYMS Belfast 1991/92. Old Wesley players from left to right:
D. Jackson, A. Blair, A. Hawe, J. Cody, R. Love, M. McArdle. (Courtesy of Ken Richardson)

practice, he was the first medical person to reach Kevin O'Higgins, Minister for Justice, after O'Higgins was shot on Booterstown Avenue.

During the First World War, James Beckett was acting honorary secretary of Old Wesley. In the field of sports, he was obviously as outstanding a personality as his nephew Samuel was in the field of literature.

When the club was re-established in 1919, they needed new grounds. In his report of the annual general meeting in September 1919, James Beckett writes that the club had arranged to become tenants of Leinster Branch, able to use the new grounds in Donnybrook (now often referred to as 'Wesley') in the hope that it would work out with Bective Rangers FC, the other tenants. In this report, he refers to the arrangement between Wanderers and Lansdowne at Lansdowne Road, mentioning that they would have to build their own pavilion and look after their share of the ground.[37]

Until they were able to build their own pavilion they were allowed to use the pavilion of the Donnybrook Lawn Tennis Club.

They play in navy shorts and white jerseys with a wide red hoop rimmed with navy across the breast with a small red wyvern on the left above that hoop and have senior, junior, under-20, youth and minis teams. In their centenary season (1991/92), Old Wesley became the first Irish rugby team to beat the Barbarians. In 2012 they started playing women's rugby.

Railway Union RFC is the first rugby club in this area that was founded in the twentieth century. As it was established in late summer 1904, it was too late for them to compete in the Junior League and Cup in that season, so their first season was 1905/06. They won the Leinster Junior Challenge Cup in 1920/21, but this must have been quite nerve-racking as the first two matches in the final against Carlow both ended in a draw. They won the third game with a goal kicked from the halfway line by E.P. Flanagan. After that they applied for senior status. When they were refused this, some of their better players left to join senior clubs. This happened in the following years again. Their most successful season was 1937/38, when they won the Junior League for the first time. Another attempt to achieve senior status in 1938 also failed, but they were allowed some matches against senior clubs, half of which they won. In 1964 they won the Spencer Cup in its inaugural year.

They have over-35s, senior, junior, youth and minis, all with men's and women's teams, with the exception of the youth section, which is for girls only as boys of that age group play rugby at school. In the rugby club family,

Railway Union RFC sports grounds.

some of the groups have nicknames: the minis are called 'Locos' (short for 'The Locomotives') and the over-35s 'Legends'. The oldest player for the Legends was Mick Dempsey, who played against Les Zespoirs of France in 2012, aged 82. Their colours are black, purple and old gold. They have players from all over Ireland and of more than a dozen nationalities.

In spring 2012, floodlights were installed for their rugby pitch.

Old Belvedere RFC was established in 1918/9 at a general meeting held in Belvedere College. At first they shared the grounds at Beech Hill, Donnybrook with Old St Mary's. The club then played in the Dublin League. At the final meeting of that year, it was decided to enter senior rugby and open the club to sister Jesuit colleges and 'to outsiders, who may wish to join', as is mentioned on their website. The first game in the Leinster Senior Cup took place against Wanderers on 17 March 1920 and was lost 0–3. Kevin Barry played in their 2nd XV in that season.

The arrest and subsequent execution of Kevin Barry, the internment of other players, including their captain, the loss of the ground in Beech Hill and the move to an inferior pitch in Vernon Avenue with the resultant loss of key players during the transition all contributed to the demise of the original club, which folded before the commencement of the 1922/3 season.

The club was reformed as a junior club in April 1930, restricted to past pupils of Belvedere College, and a new ground was leased in Ballymun.

The first trophy won was the Metropolitan Cup in 1936, which they retained in 1937. These results encouraged the club to apply for senior status, which was duly granted for the season 1937/38. The ground lease in Anglesea Road was acquired in 1944, but the first match was not played until February 1949 as the work required to level and drain the pitches took a long time. The con-

Kevin Barry (1902-1920).

crete terrace that exists today dates from 1958, the present pavilion was opened in 1962 and the old bar and ballroom were replaced in 1995 after a fire in 1993. Dr Karl Mullen, captain of the Irish rugby team that won the Grand Slam for the first time in 1948, was an active member of Old Belvedere.

Clubhouse, Old Belvedere RFC.

Daniel Riordan, Old Belvedere at Musgrave Park. (Courtesy of Old Belvedere RFC)

They play in black shorts and jerseys with black and white hoops and have senior and junior teams as well as minis.

In the 1990s, the club started playing women's rugby. They have two women's teams now and six of their players were on the Irish team for the Women's Rugby World Cup 2014, the highest number of any club.

Long before the establishment of **Leinster Rugby** as a club, the Leinster Branch of the Irish Rugby Football Union (IRFU) was inaugurated on 31 October 1879. The clubs represented at the meeting were Wanderers, Lansdowne, Arlington School, Dublin University, Dundalk, Phoenix FC and Stephen's Hospital.[38] One of the objectives of the Leinster Branch was the selection of representative teams. This was done on an ad-hoc basis and the first interprovincial match took place between Leinster and Ulster in the 1875/6 season in Lansdowne Road. Interprovincial matches were used to select the players for the national team. The four-province interprovincial championship did not start until the 1946/7 season.[39]

In 1995 Leinster became a professional rugby club under the name 'Leinster Lions'. The word 'Lions' was dropped before the 2004/5 season. Today they are known as 'Leinster Rugby' but Leo the Lion is still their mascot. At the beginning of the twenty-first century, they became one of the best European rugby teams. New players are recruited in schools and coached at U-16, U-17 and U-18 levels, leading into their 'Leinster Academy', a three-year programme to train young and promising players which has been very successful. They won the Celtic League Championship in 2002 and 2008, the European Rugby Champion Cup in 2009, 2011 and 2012, the European Rugby Challenge Cup in 2013 and the PRO12 Championship in 2013 and 2014.

Their ever-increasing supporter numbers led them to move their matches in the 2006/7 season from Donnybrook Rugby Ground to the RDS Arena. In January 2015, they announced the winner of a competition for the design of an improved and enlarged RDS Arena and that the work would start in 2016.

Leinster v. Glasgow Warriors, 1 March 2014.

Sandymount Rugby Club is not mentioned in order of date of foundation as that date is not known. It is not even known if Sandymount Rugby Club is its proper name. It must have been founded between 1880 (it is not mentioned in R.M. Peter) and the mid-1890s. What is known is that in the 1895/6 season the Leinster Branch of the IRFU started their Junior League and in the centenary publication of the Leinster Branch a club named 'Sandymount' is mentioned as one of the clubs entered for the inaugural competition in that season. The first three matches in the Junior League Competition were played on 4 January 1896. One of those matches was Sandymount v. GPO.[40]

A photograph in the pavilion of Monkstown FC shows a club with a similar name, but if the date after the name is the date of its establishment, this club cannot be the same that played in the 1895/6 season. The history of the photograph is not known.

No other information could be gathered about this club or these clubs which no longer exist. It is possible that they had an arrangement with the Sandymount Cricket Club similar to that which Monkstown Rugby and Pembroke Cricket Clubs have now, the rugby club using the grounds in winter and the cricket club in summer.[41] If that was the case, they played on the ground between Sandymount Road and the sea north of what then was Howth View and is now Marine Parade, an area that is today completely built up.

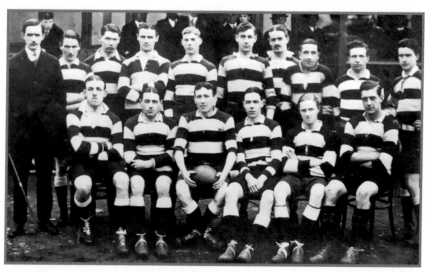

Old Sandymount RFC (1913). Junior Cup Final, February 1914. From left to right, back row: Hughton, McElland, Nichols, Clarke, Young, Gore, Watson, Grant, Roberts, O'Dwyer. Front row: Goodbody, Ramsay, Harris (Capt.), Ramsay, Little, Hill (Gore was killed in France 1915 and Grant in 1916). (Photograph courtesy of Monkstown FC)

The Battle of the High Hitters

Sandymount, 27 July 2012.

It was a dry and sunny day. The battle started at 2.30 p.m., just after lunch, and lasted most of the afternoon.

What? The battle? In Sandymount?

Of course, everybody knows there has been a famous battle in one of the suburbs of Dublin, but that was over a thousand years ago – and on the north side!

Members of the green team.

Dave Kearney, Rob Kearney, Leo Cullen and Johnny Sexton of the blue side.

Still, there we were, watching them, one side in green uniforms, the other in blue and both sides with famous officers and well-known faces in their support team.

Before they started, the green side discussed their strategy.

The blue side at that stage did not seem to be too sure yet about whom they should be sending into the battle.

Now things get clearer. They called it the 'Battle of the High Hitters', but it was a very good-natured meeting, a charity event to benefit Spinal Injuries Ireland, a Twenty20 Challenge between Cricket Ireland and Leinster Rugby. The blue squad posted an outstanding 202 from their 21 overs, with 7 pairs batting 3 overs each. The Cricket Ireland XI generously added 100 to the total they needed to chase, but their generosity was severely misplaced as the Leinster Rugby men thrived in the field and put the 'squeeze' on the men in green throughout their innings. As the photo shows, they were pleased with their win and also with the fact that this 'battle' raised over €20,000 for Spinal Injuries Ireland.

The blues were the winners.

Cricket

It is not quite clear when **Sandymount CC** was founded. It seems to have been the first cricket club in the area as it existed in the early 1860s as on 14 March 1864 *TheIrish Times* advised:

> SANDYMOUNT CRICKET CLUB. A meeting will be held at the Phoenix Hotel, D'Olier street, on this evening (Monday), at 8 o'clock, for the election of officers for the ensuing season.

In the same year, Sandymount Cricket Club played County Wicklow Cricket Club in a famous match in which the first double century was scored in Ireland by J. Gilligan. In that match, Charles Stewart Parnell captained the County Wicklow Cricket Club. Parnell's grandfather and father had been great patrons of cricket. His father John Henry Parnell, who played for Carlow and the Phoenix Club, had set up the County Wicklow Cricket Club on his Avondale Estate. Charles Stewart Parnell played for and captained Wicklow and occasionally played for the Phoenix Club, as well as leading teams against it.[42] Sandymount CC later played on the cricket grounds of Lansdowne Road for a while but folded around 1907.[43]

Pembroke CC, founded 1868, is the oldest of the cricket clubs in this area that still exist. They share a clubhouse and pitch with Monkstown

Pembroke CC and Monkstown RFC clubhouse.

Pembroke Cricket Club 3rd XI, 1960. From left to right, back row: J. Watt,
P. Fitzpatrick, J. Liston, G. Hook, S. Fitzpatrick, D. Clark. Front row: R. Dawburn,
D. Bradshaw, F. Malin (Captain), J. Campbell, J. O'Driscoll. (Courtesy of Douglas Clark)

FC. Pembroke CC fields six men's teams in league and cup competitions. They have three ladies' teams and schoolboy league teams in the under-11, under-13, under-15, under-17 and under-19 age groups. The First XI won the Leinster Senior Cup in its inaugural year, 1935, and on twelve occasions since. It has regularly provided players for the Irish national team, of whom S.F. Bergin, with fifty-three caps between 1949 and 1965, is the most famous, and the 1999 captain, Peter Davy, and his twin brother John the most recent. In 1999 Peter Davy scored 132 for Ireland against the MCC (Marylebone Cricket Club) at Lords.

The photograph of the 3rd XI of Pembroke CC in 1960 hung on the wall of the clubhouse for many years.

As the railway line runs past their pitch, DART users can occasionally watch them practise for a short time or even glimpse a moment of a match. When the field is not used by sport people and especially when the ground is wet, considerable numbers of gulls forage there for worms. Occasionally you can find oystercatchers and curlews there and in winter brent geese as well.

Lansdowne Cricket Club was founded by Henry W.D. Dunlop, like the other sport clubs branching from the Irish Champion Athletic Club in 1873. Dunlop was very eager to have a cricket club in his grounds, but the club never reached the front rank of Dublin clubs. They improved a bit at the end of the 1870s, but that did not last long. Their best player, Jack Hynes, who scored the only century on the grounds in 1884, won twenty-seven caps for Ireland. He did not only play for Lansdowne, but also for Trinity and Phoenix. Lansdowne CC disappeared in the 1890s.[44]

Pavilion, YMCA Cricket and Hockey Club.

Seán McAuley batting for the 1st XI, 2010. (Courtesy of YMCA Cricket Club)

YMCA CC is seventeen years younger, founded in 1890. They played on hired grounds until 1911, when they acquired their own pitch in Claremont Road in Sandymount. In 1930 their First XI was the Intermediate League winner. They were admitted into the senior league in 1934 and in 1955 won the Leinster Senior League for the first time. By 2013 they had won it four more times. Between 1984 and 2014, they won the Leinster Senior Cup ten times. In 2005 they moved into their new pavilion on the ground.

Apart from their senior teams, they have teams for boys and girls.

Merrion CC in Donnybrook is next by age. It can be traced back to the Land Commission CC, founded in 1892, which at first played in the Lansdowne Rugby Grounds. This club seems to have disappeared around 1900. In 1906 some members of that earlier club founded the Merrion Cricket Club, taking the name from the address of the offices of the Land Commission in 24 Upper Merrion Street. The new club took the colours of the defunct Land Commission Cricket Club: Lincoln green, maroon and gold. From its beginning, it was open to civil servants of other departments in the Merrion Street area. For two years they played in Dolphin's Barn and

Merrion Cricket Club pavilion in August 2010.

J. Morrisey Jnr. (Courtesy of Merrion CC)

Pitch, Merrion Cricket Club.

since 1908 on the ground they still occupy between Anglesea Road and the Dodder in Donnybrook. First they rented this from the Pembroke Estate, but in 1952 they bought it. In 1919 the club was opened to non-civil servants and in 1926 they were admitted to the Leinster Senior League. Since 1930 they have survived three major floodings of the River Dodder, including the one caused by hurricane Charley in 1986, as well as a fire that destroyed the club pavilion.

There were other downs, but there were great ups as well, like winning the Irish Senior Cup in 2010.

They have men's, ladies', boys' and girls' teams.

Their pitch stretches right down to the bank of the Dodder in a beautifully landscaped area.

In the second half of 2014, they were able to move into their new pavilion on the same site.

Railway Union CC was established in 1904. They have older roots as Railway Union goes back to an initiative of employees of the Irish Railway Clearing House (IRCH). This organisation had a cricket club that played in the Junior Cup competition in the 1902/03 season. Railway Union CC started to play on the grounds of Valentine Whelan's dairy farm. The Whelan family stayed involved in the cricket club to this day; Heather Whelan captains not only the Railway Union ladies' cricket team but the Irish ladies' cricket team as well. In 1911 Railway Union Cricket Club was promoted to senior rank. There were no leagues as yet, but their 2nd XI won the Intermediate Cup in 1918, and in 1919 they were a founder member of the Leinster Senior League. During the 1930s, they were relegated to junior rank, but returned to senior rank in 1945.

In the late 1950s, their schoolboys, most of them from Sandymount, won the leagues at all age levels (Brendan 'Ginger' O'Brien was one of them) and in 1960 Railway Union CC won the senior league, as they did in 1962. The Leinster Senior Cup followed in 1967.

Since the 1940s, they have ladies' teams, which have been especially successful since the 1980s. One player, Nikki Squire, won thirty-seven Irish caps and captained Ireland six times, including the team of the European Cup in 2001 when they won all three of their games. The Irish team repeated their success in 2009 under their captain Heather Whelan.

The club has quite a few loyal families, both 'vertically', with up to four generations of the same family, as well as 'horizontally', with six brothers Behan for instance or five brothers and one sister O'Brien playing more or less at the same time and playing well: Niall O'Brien won the Leinster Cricket Union (LCU) Young Player Award in 2002 and his younger brother

Railway Union CC in a match. (Courtesy of Railway Union CC)

Kevin O'Brien, here in the jersey of Cricket Ireland. (With kind permission of Kevin O'Brien)

Kevin won the same award in 2003, the year in which their father Brendan 'Ginger' O'Brien, who had captained the Irish team in his time, was awarded the LCU Hall of Fame Award. Niall and Kevin played in the Irish National Team that in March 2011 beat England in the World Cup; the younger, Kevin O'Brien, deciding that historic match. Since then he holds the world record for the fastest century ever scored at a World Cup.

Niall O'Brien was a member of the Irish team that beat the West Indies in the World Cup Pool B game in Nelson in February 2015.

Hockey

Hockey seems to have arrived in Dublin 4 somewhat later than rugby and cricket.

Three Rock Rovers Hockey Club, the oldest hockey club in this area, was founded in the 1893/94 season by graduates of Dublin University and members of the University Hockey Club. The club initially played at grounds in Foxrock before they moved to one of the Irish international venues, the grounds of the Irish Hockey Union at Londonbridge Road. From 1929 they shared the grounds with Lansdowne Lawn Tennis Club. In 1981 Three Rock Rovers sold the Londonbridge Road Grounds and moved out of the area to Grange Road in Rathfarnham.

The club was Ireland's entrant in the 2008 EuroHockey League. In the final of the Irish Senior Cup (ISC), Three Rock Rovers beat Pembroke Wanderers on penalty strokes to win the ISC for the first time in forty years in February 2014.

They have six senior teams for men and five for women, apart from men's and women's veterans and a junior team each for boys and girls.

Railway Union Hockey Club, whose men's team was established in 1904, is the oldest hockey club still in the area. They were promoted to senior status in 1912 and won the Leinster Senior League eleven years running from 1922 to 1933 and again in 1949 and 1967. In 1990 the club got a new AstroTurf pitch.

Arguably the most outstanding player for Railway Union was Joey A. O'Meara, who captained the 1st XI for many years, received fifty-five caps for Ireland and captained the Irish team that won the eight nations' tournament in Santander, Spain, beating England in the final in 1972. He played for Railway Union for thirty-two years.

Railway Union's Kenny Carroll is one of the few sportsmen to have been capped for Ireland in two sports: cricket and hockey. He plays both in Railway Union.

The original hockey pitch of Railway Union is the only part not owned by the club; it is leased from the Sisters of Charity whereas the ground rent for the rest of the ground was bought out in October 1987.

In 1985 a Colts' League was introduced by the Leinster branch of the Irish Hockey Association and Railway Union Hockey Club started in that

Kenny Carroll, Railway Union Hockey Club and Railway Union Cricket Club.
(Courtesy of Adrian Boehm/Irish Hockey Photographers and with kind permission of Kenny Carroll)

group with under-12, under-14 and under-16 teams. They now have under-8 and under-10 teams as well.

In 1980 the Ireland v. England international was played on Railway Union ground. In 2014 and 2015, the men's team represented Ireland at the EuroHockey Indoor Club Champions Challenge.

The ladies' section was formed in 1919 with seventeen members and one team. In 1942 they were promoted to senior status. Eighty-five years after their foundation they have eighty-five players and field five teams. In 1985 their Colts' section was formed and in 1990 they were one of the founders of Leinster Ladies Veterans' hockey. Since the mid-1960s, quite a few of their members have played on the Irish national team, both at senior and junior levels. In 2014 the ladies' hockey team won the bronze medal in the EuroHockey Club Trophy Championship.

They have a tradition of umpiring at all levels up to International Hockey Federation (FIH) level. As in the men's section, many members have served in the administration of Irish and Leinster hockey.

YMCA Hockey Club in Claremont Road, Sandymount, was founded 1908. They are one of the largest men's hockey clubs in Ireland with veteran, senior, under-21 and junior teams. Since 2006 they also have ladies' teams in the senior and junior sections.

The men have won the Leinster Senior League eleven times, the Irish Senior Cup five times and the Irish Junior Cup once.

Ladies of YMCA Hockey Club in action. (Courtesy of YMCA Hockey Club)

Muckross Hockey Club was founded in 1918 by past pupils of Muckross College, where they had their first ground. When Muckross College expanded they had to move. From early in the twenty-first century, they played at the Teresian School, still in Donnybrook, but at the other end of the village, a good distance from their spiritual home. In late summer 2014, they finally moved back to Muckross College Park.

Muckross Hockey Club's roll of honour is one of the most decorated in Irish club hockey with over thirty Leinster league titles, an unparalleled twenty-nine Leinster Senior (Jacqui Potter) Cup wins, a strong represen-tation at international level and a record seven past players inducted into the IHA (Irish Hockey Association) Hall of Fame. Their member Sandra O'Gorman was one of the best international goalkeepers in the world and won the award for Outstanding Goalie of the 1994 World Cup.[45] They are currently fielding six teams across different divisions in the Leinster League.

Pembroke Wanderers Hockey Club during a match on their
pitch with their pavilion in the background.

Pembroke Wanderers *v.* Clontarf, 27 February 2012. (Courtesy of Pembroke Wanderers HC)

Pembroke Wanderers Hockey Club was founded in 1922. Their pitch and clubhouse adjoin the Sandymount DART Station, which is the reason for the fence in the photograph. They have occupied the same pitch since they were founded.

They have senior teams for men and ladies as well as junior teams for different age groups. Occasionally it is possible to watch them practise or see a moment of a match from the station platform.

Their men's team won the European Champion Cup in Prague in 2007 and the EuroHockey Cup Trophy in 2009 in Dublin, four times the All-Ireland Club Championship, the Irish Hockey League in 2009, six times the Irish Senior Cup, nine times the Irish Junior Cup, seventeen times the Leinster Senior League and nineteen times the Leinster Senior Cup. Five of their players have been capped for Ireland.

The ladies won the Irish Senior Cup a dozen times, the Irish Junior Cup ten times, the Irish Junior League once, the Leinster Senior League seventeen times and the Leinster Senior Cup eight times.

GAA and Soccer

GAA

Today there is only one GAA club in the area of Dublin 4. This was not always so.

Clanna Gael-Fontenoy GAA Club is a club with many roots. It includes more clubs than those mentioned in the name (see Table 4). According to their club history, some of those formerly independent clubs were rather short-lived, others appeared, disappeared and re-appeared and others again were rivals for a long time before they finally merged. Sandymount GFC, for instance, started playing in 1903. The Pembroke Estate Papers mention some leases concerning them:

3/12/1908	Agreement to lease Prescott and Henehie of use of a field off Gilford Rd., ... for use of Sandymount football club. Rent: £1 for 4 months
24/11/1909	Ditto
30/11/1910	Ditto
29/11/1911	Ditto
12/1912	Agreement to lease Gilling and Justice. Ditto
01/1915	Agreement to lease Dowling. Ditto. Rent: £ 2.10.0 for 2 months[46]

There is no lease record for them between December 1912 and January 1915, and after 1915 Sandymount GFC seems to have disappeared. In the mid-1930s, however, it re-appeared under the name Sandymount H. and F. Club and was mentioned off and on until at least 1950. Kevin Barry GFC seems to have existed only for a few seasons. Donnybrook Davitts was another short-lived club. It was first founded in 1916, but did not survive very long; it was re-founded around the turn of the millennium, again not surviving on its own for long.

Some of the early clubs had problems with membership and/or finances, others with GAA headquarters. Isles of the Sea in Ringsend were mentioned as winning the County Club Championship in 1890. In 1894 they amalgamated with the Sons of the Sea, another Ringsend GFC, and took the new name 'St Patrick's' only to revert to the old name 'Isles of the Sea' the following year. Not much later, they seemed to have disappeared and were re-founded 1899 or 1900, to become All-Ireland Football Champions in 1901. Later that year, they had problems with GAA headquarters, with the result that some of their members left the GAA and joined the newly founded soccer club Shamrock Rovers in

Sandymount GFC, 1905. From left to right, back row: T. Mullany, P. Smith (Vice-President), J. Kirwan, J. Mullaney, P. Byrne, C. Mullany, M. Williams, D. O'Ryan (Vice-President). Middle row: T. Powers, S.D. White (President), P. Henderson, J. Daly, E. Ennis, P. Roe, J. Byrne, J. Malone, J. Sandford (Hon. Treasurer). Front row: W. O'Byrne (Hon. Secretary), Jas. Power, J. Byrne, J. Carroll (Captain), J. Kemple, W. Carpenter, Jos Power (Vice-Captain). (Courtesy of Clanna Gael-Fontenoy GAA Club)

Irishtown Road. Isles of the Sea broke up in 1903 and were re-organised in 1906 and in 1912.

Some old photographs show teams of clubs that later merged into the one club of today, such as that on p.67. It is possible that the 'E. Ennis' mentioned in the middle row is the chimney cleaner Edward Ennis (b. 1883) of Dromard Avenue, Sandymount, who was killed on Easter Monday 1916 and after whom Ennis Grove off Londonbridge Road is named.

Originally those clubs played wherever there was a free field in their area. Fontenoy first had grounds in Bath Avenue and later played in Herbert Park; from July 1910 then they used no. 5 pitch in Ringsend Park. From May 1911, matches of Sandymount GFC are also reported to have been played in Ringsend Park. Some other GAA clubs played in a field off Gilford Road, others on the grounds of St Benburb's FC on Beech Hill at the border between Donnybrook and Clonskeagh (roughly where the Riverview Leisure Centre is now). Other pitches could be even further away. One of the constituents of the modern club, Clanna Gaedhel (now Clanna Gael) was the GFC of (former) students of St Patrick's Teacher Training College Drumcondra, another, 'Peadar Mackens', is mentioned in 1937 as having new grounds in Windy Arbour.

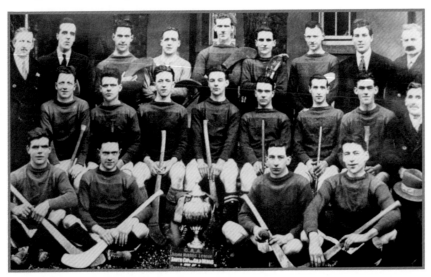

Fontenoy GAC, 1927. From left to right, back row: Martin Kennedy, J. Carroll (Treasurer), Patrick Maguire, Mick Nolan, John Condron, Paddy Cleary, John Fitzharris, Frank Geoghegan, Jos Fletcher (Sr). Middle row: Jack Clifford, Phil Cleary, Simon Murphy, Willie Murray, Joe Greene, Frank Keegan, Larry Fitzpatrick, Mick Tobin. Front row: Dinny Cleary, Willie Maguire, Leo Rossiter, Jim Murphy. (Courtesy of Clanna Gael-Fontenoy GAA Club)

Clanna Gaedhel, the club of student teachers of St Patrick's in Drumcondra, had members from all over the country. A team list of theirs in a local 1936 contest (Dublin Senior Football Championship) reads:

O'Hara (Laoighis), Ruane (Westmeath), Whitty (Kerry), Kenny (Dublin), Feeney (Waterford), Dowling (Kildare), O'Driscoll (Dublin), McAuliffe (Cork), Gorman (Kerry), Sheehan (Cork), Keaney (Leitrim), Brosnan (Kerry), Conlan (Armagh), O'Dowd (Kerry), V. White (Cavan), A. Fitzpatrick (Kildare), sub.[47]

They entered the contest as a local Dublin team, but only two of the players were originally from Dublin.

Clanna Gael-Fontenoy GAA Club's website includes a very interesting section about their history.[48] The following additional information was provided by their club manager, Shay Connolly:

Clubs went out of business more than them all amalgamating. Peadar Mackens folded sometime in the late fifties and I never heard of anything from Sandymount FC or HC after this period. When Peadar Mackens folded most of their players went to play for Clanna Gael. Clanna Gael started a Juvenile section in the early sixties in both football and hurling in the Ringsend/Sandymount area and Fontenoy were continuing to draw from this same caption [sic] area. These were the only two GAA clubs left in the area at the time.

As it was becoming very divisive for the clubs to be vying against each other they both amalgamated in 1969. The amalgamation went very smooth [sic] and both clubs worked very hard at this coalition. It is firmly one club now.

The club was in grave danger of going to the wall in the 1980s but recovered to build the club it is today with over thirty teams in existence. All other Dublin Inner City Clubs have folded since the 1960s.

Since 1910 Fontenoy teams played in Ringsend Park and they still play there, in addition to their grounds in Seán Moore Park, where they built a clubhouse in 1988. Not very much later, this had become too small, so in 2002 they added an extension, which is bigger than the original clubhouse. They now have nearly fifty teams, providing possibilities for football for men and women, as well as hurling and camogie for different age groups. They also have a vibrant nursery academy, which caters for boys and girls up to the age of 6, introducing them to GAA sports.

Ladies' football. (Courtesy of Clanna Gael-Fontenoy and with kind permission of Aisling M. Ryan)

In the first years, Fontenoy seem to have played Gaelic football only, with the first match recorded in October 1887 on grounds at Elm Park where St Vincent's Hospital is now. Fontenoy Hurling Club was affiliated to the Dublin County Board in 1901 and the first indication of a match is in an official note written the same year calling players to their playing ground in Londonbridge Road.

For many years, Clanna Gael-Fontenoy have worked together with the Star of the Sea National School in Sandymount. Now they are also hosts for the GAA teams of Trinity College, Dublin, as they are conveniently near and have space that TCD does not have. They are sponsored by Dublin Port Company.

Soccer

Soccer is a favourite sport in the northern half of Dublin 4. Many of the soccer clubs in the area have their base in the villages of Ringsend and Irishtown and the northern part of Ballsbridge, especially in the townlands Beggars' Bush and East and North Baggotrath. They build on a much older history of soccer in this neighbourhood, but nearly all the soccer clubs still in this area are younger than the rugby clubs here.

Liffey Wanderers was established in 1883, the same year in which the Dublin University AFC was founded. This latter club insists that it is the oldest extant Dublin soccer club. Many generations of the same families have played for Liffey Wanderers over the decades. On a number of occasions, the football club came close to extinction but every time it was rescued by dedicated club volunteers. Over the years, Liffey recruited many ex-schoolboy footballers from the soccer club Pearse Rangers. For that reason, it seemed sensible for the clubs to amalgamate in 2006. The amalgamation, however, did not go as planned and in 2010 each club went its own way again. Liffey Wanderers are now based in Irishtown Stadium and play in the Leinster Senior League. In May 2015, they won their first FAI Junior Cup, with the final played in the Aviva Stadium, and followed this up by winning the Leinster Senior League Major Sunday Division shortly afterwards.

Freebooters FC was a soccer club of Sandymount. They were set up in the 1890s as a club for young Irish Catholic men that were educated in English Catholic colleges.[49] In 1900 the club lost the Leinster Senior Cup Final match played against local rivals Shelbourne FC. Their highest achievement was reaching the Irish Cup Final in 1901, which was staged at the City and County Grounds, Jones Road, Dublin, now Croke Park. Freebooters had beaten Linfield FC in the semi-final at the Jones Road venue, but in the first Irish Cup Final played outside Belfast they lost to Cliftonville FC.

Freebooters' Grounds were on Sandymount Road where Seafort Gardens are now. The grounds had previously been leased by the Catholic University Medical School and before that it was referred to as Army Grounds. The Freebooters' club was made up of players from families such as the O'Reillys, the McCanns and the Meldons, who also were keen cricket players.[50]

In 1906 Shelbourne FC began playing their home games on these grounds as Freebooters went into decline. Even after Shelbourne became tenants, the grounds were still referred to as Freebooters' Grounds.

Two of the best-known soccer clubs in Dublin were founded in this area: Shelbourne FC and Shamrock Rovers. Both have moved out of Dublin 4, but their history started here and they still have a huge fan base in the area.

Shelbourne FC, known as 'Shels', was founded in 1895 in the Bath Avenue area and took its name from nearby Shelbourne Road. In 1896/7 they won the Leinster Junior Cup, in 1897/8 they reached the Leinster Senior Cup final and in 1902/3 they won the Leinster Senior League, winning it again the following year and adding the Leinster Senior Cup to it. In 1905 they turned 'professional' in the sense that at least some players were paid: the first player paid by the club, James Wall, got a halfpenny per week if he played. In 1906 they became the first southern club to win the IFA (Irish Football Association) Cup. They repeated this in 1911 and 1920. But 1921 saw the split between the IFA for the six northern counties and the FAI (Football Association of Ireland) for the Free State. In this year Shelbourne FC became a founder member of the League of Ireland.

As Shelbourne played most of their matches on Saturdays and not Sundays, like other clubs, they were sometimes called 'The Protestant Club', but more often 'The Dockers' Club' as many of their players worked as dockers, pointing to the fact that soccer was a sport for the working class.

They first played on waste grounds in the Bath Avenue/Havelock Square area but they used these grounds only in their first season. In their second season they used a pitch on Claremont Road and in their third season one in Park Avenue before moving for three seasons to Beaver Row, where the Riverview Leisure Centre is now.

Donnybrook at that time seems to have been a bit too far for their fans from the Ringsend/Irishtown/Sandymount area and so new grounds were sought. For four seasons, their home grounds were on Serpentine Avenue before they moved, in 1906, to Sandymount Road into the ground of Freebooters FC, a club which had gone into decline. The 1907 OS map shows a 'Shelbourne Park Football Ground' on the same spot that the Sandymount Cricket and Sandymount Rugby Club, mentioned earlier, had used. This ground was also called 'Freebooters' Grounds'. The 1907 OS map shows that it had a stand. Shels stayed there until 1913, when they finally moved across the Dodder in Ringsend to the stadium that today still has their name.

Shelbourne FC stayed in Shelbourne Park until 1949, sharing the stadium with the greyhounds from 1927 onwards. Between 1949 and 1989, their first team moved around (including playing for one season in Irishtown Stadium) before settling in Tolka Park in Drumcondra, where they still are. They used Irishtown Stadium for practice and junior-team matches until the 1970s, so more than half their history was in the Pembroke Township/Dublin 4 area. At home they play in red and white, away in shades of blue.

Until 2011 Shelbourne was the only Irish team to reach the third qualifying round of the UEFA Champions League, where they were beaten by Deportivo La Coruña of Galicia, Spain 3–0 on aggregate in 2004.

Philly Hughes of Shelbourne FC in action against Shamrock Rovers, 23 March 2012.
(Courtesy of Maurice Frazer)

Apart from their senior teams, Shelbourne have seventeen schoolboy teams competing in the Dublin & District Schoolboy Leagues (DDSL) and an amateur team in the Amateur Football League (AFL).

Shamrock Rovers Football Club was formed in 1901 after a meeting of soccer enthusiasts in Ringsend. However, the gates of their long-time home, Glenmalure Park, claimed that the founding year was 1899.[51] Their websites says:

> The very first meeting took place at number four Irishtown Road but it wasn't until the second meeting was held around the corner in Shamrock Avenue that the name Shamrock Rovers was decided upon.[52]

Local historians have always regarded the street named 'Watery Lane' in 1868, 'Riverview Avenue' in 1907 and 'Dermot O'Hurley Avenue' today as the border between Ringsend and Irishtown. Shamrock Avenue disappeared sometime during the last century, but it is shown on old maps, slightly north of the Irishtown/Ringsend border in the area that now is called 'The Square'. Bath Avenue is in the townland in Beggars' Bush, which is now regarded to be the southern border of Irishtown, so the two opponents in the photograph above were originally near neighbours before one of them moved north of the Liffey and the other to South County Dublin.

It was not until the break-up of the Gaelic football club Isles of the Sea in 1903 that Shamrock Rovers really took off, with many Gaelic footballers switching their allegiance to soccer and becoming members of Shamrock Rovers.

In their early years, Shamrock Rovers played in green and white stripes, but, inspired by the clubs Celtic FC in Glasgow and Belfast, they changed their kit in 1927 to a hooped design in the same colours. This is why, like Celtic in Glasgow, they are known as 'The Hoops'. They joined the Leinster Football Association shortly after the formation of the club in 1901 and, having won league and cup honours as members of the County Dublin League, they advanced up the ranks to the Leinster Senior League (LSL). However, as they could not secure the private pitch necessary to take part in the LSL they were forced to withdraw from official football. In 1914 they were revived and joined the Leinster Junior League. After a further short spell in the LSL in 1916, they had to withdraw again, but Rovers finally got up and running in 1920 when they joined the Leinster Junior League. Within two years, they became members of the newly formed League of

Ireland in the 1922/23 season and haven't looked back since. Their first own grounds were in Windy Arbour, but they played many of their home games in Ringsend Park.

In the 1920s, the club moved to Glenmalure Park, Milltown Road, Dublin 6, upon joining the League of Ireland, but continued to draw most of their support from Ringsend, Irishtown and Sandymount. In 1926 Shamrock Rovers moved from their first pitch at Milltown to another one, which was located just behind the original grounds. From then on, they developed their grounds, building covered stands and terracing. For their big matches, crowds of up to 30,000 were often recorded. During their sixty-five-year tenure at Glenmalure Park, the Hoops earned the reputation of being Ireland's most successful club, winning every trophy at domestic level and taking on the giants of European football. The club suffered a major catastrophe in 1987 when the then owners removed them from Milltown in order to develop the land for commercial purposes. After twenty-two years of wandering around the city, which included six years in the RDS (1990–1996), as well as playing their home games at the grounds of their rivals, Shamrock Rovers finally settled into a home of their own again when they took up residence at Tallaght Stadium in 2009.

Although now based in Dublin 24, Shamrock Rovers still retain a sizeable fan base in the Dublin 4 region. Shamrock Rovers think it appropriate that their present grounds are situated adjacent to the River Dodder, which runs down from the mountains and then through Tallaght as well as Milltown and along the RDS before entering the Liffey at Ringsend, all places that have connections with the Rovers.

In the summer of 2010, Shamrock Rovers reached the second round of the Europa League qualification process. They hosted Juventus Turin, but they were beaten 3–0 on aggregate. One year later, they reached the group level of the Europa League, winning against Partizan Belgrade 3–2 on aggregate. Unluckily they did not manage to get any further then, but that might still come.

Today, Shamrock Rovers not only have a senior team, but also an Under-21 team, an intermediate team, sixteen schoolboy teams, a senior ladies' team and three schoolgirl teams.

Railway Union FC was established in 1904, like all Railway Union clubs, but it built on the foundations of teams of the IRCH (Irish Railway Clearing House), which had played in the 1902/03 season, and the GNR (Great Northern Railway). In October 1904, Railway Union FC was a founder member of the Athletic Union League (AUL), which they won in the first season. In 1905 they joined the Leinster Junior League, but returned to the AUL after only eight matches. In 1906 they were elected to the Leinster Senior League Division II but they kept their Second XI in the AUL and in 1920 reverted completely to the AUL. From 1938 to 1972, they had to play their home matches away from the Railway Union site in Park Avenue as they were asked to give up their pitch to help the Railway Union RFC get senior status. During that time, they first played in Railway Union's second grounds at Clonskeagh and later in Shelbourne Stadium and Chapelizod. In 1946/47, after the Second World War and a year without any team, they entered Leinster Senior League Division I, but soon had to return to junior football. In 1954 the club was a founder member of the Dublin Amateur Football League (DAFL, now AFL) but in 1956 they were back in the AUL. In 1971 they returned 'home' to Park Avenue and entered the Leinster Senior League, which they had to leave again in the 1995/96 season due to a lack of staff. After absorbing South Dock Celtic FC in the first years of the new millennium, they rejoined the Leinster Senior League as Railway Union FC. Currently they have a strong interest in young players, with ten teams from the under-7s to the under-18s in the DDSL (Dublin and District Schoolboys League) and SDFL (South Dublin Football League). Their senior team plays in the Athletic Union League again.

St Mark's Athletic FC was founded in St Mark's parish, from which it took its name. The parish history is not certain about the founding date; the earliest date mentioned is 1892.[53] This is confirmed in another parish history that states that since the closure of St Mark's church, St Mark's Athletic FC, whose roots go back as far as 1892, had its headquarters in St Stephen's parochial hall.[54]

This refers to the parochial hall of St Stephen's parish on Northumberland Road. St Mark's Athletic FC itself gives 1906 as the year in which it was established. They practically ceased to exist between 1914 and 1918 as it is reported that they joined the forces almost to a man. In the forces, they played many friendly matches to keep themselves in training.[55] By 1922 they were back in form.

According to *Poyntz*, they played in the Athletic Union League and the United Churches League in the mid-1970s. Now they play in the Amateur Football League Dublin (AFL). They play in Ringsend Park (pitch no. 5 is their home pitch), but may also use Irishtown Stadium.

Tritonville FC seems to have been short-lived. It is not recorded when they were established, but they were in existence in 1906. Their reputation was not the best and in 1906 senior clubs in Belfast asked the IFA to prevent Tritonville FC from entering the Irish Cup. One of the reasons given was that their players were too brutal.[56]

For the season 1912/13, they competed in the Irish League. This was the only season in which three Dublin clubs did so (the others were Shelbourne and Bohemians). Tritonville held the last (tenth) position and did not appear in the tables again.[57] They played on a pitch that the GAA used for matches on Sundays. This created problems with the IFA (Irish Football Association), which was based in Belfast, and in 1906 Ulster delegates brought in a motion that IFA-affiliated clubs that played on pitches 'on which Sunday sports or Gaelic football are held' would be expelled from senior competition. Leinster delegates managed to amend this. In 1912 Tritonville started to use the grounds that were both known as 'Freebooters' Grounds' and as 'Shelbourne Park'. In 1912, they shared their pitch with Shelbourne FC. It could not be determined at what time they ceased to exist.

Pearse Rangers were originally established in the 1930s and enjoyed great success on the soccer pitch, culminating in 1960 when the football club won the FAI Junior Cup and the AUL Division 1.

The 'old' Pearse Rangers in the 1940s. (Courtesy of Pearse Rangers FC)

At some time after this, the club went out of existence only to be re-formed in 1988 to provide a schoolboy football club for the local area. The club built up its membership to such an extent that it was ultimately able to field ten teams, ranging in age from 7 to 17.[58] From 2006 until 2010, they were amalgamated with Liffey Wanderers under the name Liffeys Pearse. After the two clubs split up, Pearse Rangers, with the address PARC in Pearse House, are concentrating on schoolboy football again, playing in the Dublin and District Schoolboys League. Their home games are held in Ringsend Park and they still get lots of their players from the Ringsend and Irishtown area.

St Patrick's CY FC was formed in 1936 as St Patrick's Catholic Young Men's Society, Ringsend Branch (St Patrick's CYMS). The society is now called Catholic Men & Women's Society of Ireland (CMWS). In 1984 the club changed its name to St Patrick's CYFC. They won the FAI Junior Cup in 1946 and 1979 and the Leinster Junior Cup in 1987. In 2013 they won the John Tynan Cup and were finalists for the Joe Gilligan Cup. St Pat's has three senior teams playing in the Leinster Senior League (LSL) and also provides schoolboy football. They play both in Irishtown Stadium and Ringsend Astro Park.

St Patrick's CYFC before the Leinster Senior Cup final against Shamrock Rovers in Tallaght, September 2012. (Courtesy St Patrick's CYFC)

For some amateur clubs, it did not seem possible to source more information than is given here, despite trying different venues.

Ballsbridge FC plays in the Amateur Football League (AFL). Their home pitch is no. 1 pitch in Herbert Park.

Irishtown FC plays in the AFL. For their home matches, they use pitch no. 4 in Ringsend Park.

Bath Markievicz Celtic FC is an amalgamation of three clubs, of which one takes the name from Bath Avenue in Beggars' Bush townland, now regarded as the border between Irishtown and Sandymount. The club is based in Ringsend. They used to play in the Leinster Senior League (LSL) but now play in the Dublin and District Schoolboys League (DDSL) and are known as Markievicz Celtic.

Cambridge Boys FC is based in Ringsend, Dublin. Named after Cambridge Avenue, the soccer club was established in 1969. Cambridge has catered for the football needs of hundreds of schoolboys from Ringsend and the surrounding areas for over four decades. They have a connection with Stella Maris Rowing Club as both of them have some roots in the Cambridge Athletic Club, established in 1932. They play in the DDSL, using pitches in Ringsend Park.

Ringsend Rovers FC was started in 1970 by a committee of two. Its aims were to keep the local youth from getting into mischief, as well as encouraging them to play football seriously. They had no grounds of their own and no changing rooms, but they won the Leinster Junior League in 1975/76 nevertheless. Now they play in the Leinster Senior League (LSL).

South Dock Celtic FC was established at the end of the twentieth century and based in Ringsend, where in 2002 they got a grant of €1,500 to purchase training equipment from the CDPI (Community Development Project Initiative).[59] Not much later they became affiliated to Railway Union FC and played one season still under their own name. After that they stopped appearing as an independent club.

Belmont FC in Donnybrook was founded in 1982. They do not have a club-house of their own and play their home matches in Herbert Park. Belmont is a football club for schoolboys and -girls and has teams from under-7 to under-16. They subscribe to the view that fair play is a way of thinking, not just behaving. Their league is the South Dublin Football League (SDFL), which caters for schoolboys and -girls from the ages of 7 to 18.

Beechwood FC is a schoolboy football club in Donnybrook that was founded in 1996. The club plays in the SDFL, with teams that start with under-7. They play their home games on the grounds of the Royal Hospital Donnybrook: Herbert Park and Alexandra College, Milltown, Dublin.

Donnybrook FC was established in 2010 by two coaches specialising in coaching school children. They believe that underage football should be non-competitive and their players should be playing to have fun and make new friends. They do not grade their players as they believe that all their teams should be mixed-ability. They have teams of under-9, under-10, under-11 and under-12 and play in the DDSL; their pitch is no. 3 pitch on Herbert Park.

Racquet Sports

Tennis

Lansdowne LTC was founded in 1875 by Henry Wallace Doveton Dunlop, together with other sport clubs. He named it the 'All Ireland Lawn Tennis Club', which in 1880 was changed to 'Lansdowne Lawn Tennis Club'. It is the oldest lawn tennis club that still exists in the area and was originally located in what later became the Lansdowne Rugby Grounds. In 1929 they moved from there to the grounds of the Irish Hockey Union and Three Rock Rovers Hockey Club in Londonbridge Road.

Lansdowne LTC clubhouse beside the Dodder with
St Matthew's and Irishtown Garda station in the background.

Lansdowne LTC Ladies' Double. (Courtesy of Lansdowne LTC and with kind permission of Grace Comerford and Louise Carmody)

In 1981 Three Rock Rovers Hockey Club sold them the grounds and moved to Grange Road in Rathfarnham, since then Lansdowne LTC is the sole user of the grounds.

The sport historian Gerard Siggins regards one of their members, Joshua Pim, as the greatest Irish tennis player of all. Pim won two men's single titles at Wimbledon (1893 and 1894) and participated in two more finals (1891 and 1892), which he lost.[60] Together with his clubmate Francis Owen Stoker (known as Frank), who was a cousin of Bram Stoker of *Dracula* fame, Pim also won the double in Wimbledon in 1890 and 1893.[61] Apart from being a good tennis player, Frank Stoker also excelled at rugby and was capped five times for Ireland, which makes him one of two Irish rugby internationals who have won Wimbledon (the other one is James C. Parke of Monkstown FC).

Donnybrook LTC was founded in 1893. Their grounds are opposite Donnybrook Rugby Grounds. The Merrion Lawn Tennis Club – of which no other information could be found – offered to sell them their pavilion, roller, lawnmower, marker, nets and posts, etc., on favourable terms. The offer was accepted. Three consecutive Earls of Pembroke were presidents of the club from 1894 to 1927.[62]

When the club was founded, Donnybrook was still a village in a very rural area. The centenary book of the club mentions that during the winter a flock of sheep relieved the groundsman from mowing the grass and brought the club a 10-shilling grazing fee as well.

Though the focus of the club is social tennis, they are also great in competitions and their junior development programme is renowned for producing players of national and international quality. Each year they play host to some of Ireland's premier tennis events: for instance, the International Tennis Federation Junior World Ranking Tournament or the Irish Close Tennis Championships.

Donnybrook LTC courts and pavilion.

The club now known as **Claremont Railway Union LTC** has two roots. Railway Union Tennis Club was founded 1904, like all the other sport clubs of Railway Union. After the Second World War, Railway Tennis Club toured Sligo and Waterford and at home received the British Railway Athletic Association as well as the Ulster Transport Sports Association. The club was well known for their 'At Home' and 'Open Week'. For their diamond jubilee, they hosted a tournament of local clubs.

Claremont LTC was founded 1908. In the 1930s, a large proportion of its players were former students of UCD and Trinity. Ronald Michael (Ronnie) Delany, the Irish gold medallist of the 1956 Melbourne Olympics, played there as a junior and won the Under-19 Boys Championship in 1951. In 1972 he was captain of the club.

The two clubs merged in 1982, with the chief objective being to bring all-weather tennis to both of them. More than forty years earlier, Claremont LTC had played with the idea of acquiring more ground to lay hard courts. This was finally achieved with the merger. The hard courts were opened in 1984.

In the 1980s and '90s, the club travelled to Wexford, Rushbrook, Mullingar and Galway. At home they regularly make their courts available to neighbouring clubs who host a competition. They themselves organised tournaments over a number of seasons to raise funds for GOAL.

Apart from Delany, other eminent members of Claremont Railway Union LTC were Tommy Burke and Tristan Farren Mahon, who both represented Ireland in tennis at international level.

A new generation starting for Claremont Railway Union LTC.

The club has a thriving junior section.

Their less-used courts often serve as feeding ground for gulls and other birds.

From 1881 to 1921, **Bective LTC** was part of Bective Rangers FC. In 1921 they formally split and Bective LTC was established as a separate club, but it remains a next-door neighbour of the rugby club, with its courts between Donnybrook Rugby Grounds (home of the Rangers) and the Dodder.

Their grounds were flooded several times, the worst floods caused by Hurricane Charley in 1986. Subsequent resurfacing means that now they have a hard-court surface. They also got floodlighting, allowing play all-year round. Bective members Joe Hackett and Jim Buckley represented Ireland in the Davis Cup more than once. Hackett had his Davis Cup debut in 1950 and represented Ireland many times; he later captained the Irish team. Buckley's debut was 1959.

Elm Park LTC, established in 1926 as part of the golf and sport club, was the last tennis club established in Pembroke Township before this was incorporated into Dublin City. They have lawn courts for the summer and hard courts for all-year round. Their hard courts were upgraded during the last decade.

In 1937 they hosted the Irish Hardcourt Championships for the first time and after that for the next fourteen years.

They have and had members in Irish international teams: from 1947 on Joe McHale, J.J. Fitzgibbon, Peter Ledbetter, Robin Gibney, Ken Fitzgibbon (son of J.J. Fitzgibbon) and Robbie Dolan among the men; Patricia O'Gorman, Helen Lennon, Anne-Marie Hogan and Jenny Claffey among the women.

St Mary's LTC was founded 1947/48 by past pupils of St Mary's College in Rathmines and membership was originally confined to past pupils and members of the rugby club with associate lady members. They first played in Kenilworth Square, Dublin 6, but their membership grew so much that in 1954 they moved to Belmont Villas, Donnybrook, buying the grounds of Percy LTC. In the early 1980s, they upgraded to all-weather courts, which were re-surfaced in 2009.

Their predecessor, **Percy LTC**, had opened in 1908 with six grass courts and a croquet lawn. But in 1954 they sold their grounds to St Mary's LTC and no further information about them could be found.

Badminton

Badminton is regarded as the fastest game in the world.

Epworth Badminton Club, Sandymount was founded in 1921. They have men's, ladies' and mixed teams. They describe themselves as a small friendly club with a family feeling. They have one court and approximately thirty members. In summer they practise once a week and in winter twice a week in the evening in Christchurch Hall at Sandymount Green. The club is affiliated to the Leinster branch of the Badminton Union of Ireland and plays in the Dublin and District Leagues and Cups.

ESB Badminton Club has been in existence for more than thirty years and caters for all levels of ability. They have eleven teams (men's, ladies' and mixed) that compete in the Dublin and District Leagues, ranging from Division 4 to Division 10. They have had many successes over the years. The winter club runs on Tuesday, Thursday and Saturday nights from September to May in the Sportsco hall. The summer club runs on Thursday nights only. Coaching is available early in the winter season. They hold club competitions in September and April. Social activities include treasure hunts and weekends away.

League and Cup matches are held on Tuesdays, with Thursdays and Saturdays reserved for general play.

Table Tennis

Railway Union Table Tennis Club was established in 1931 and still existed at the golden anniversary of Railway Union in 1954, but it has disappeared since then. In the club history written for the centenary in 2004 table tennis is not mentioned.

Table tennis seems to have been popular in the parishes of the area. Milne mentions in his history of St Bartholomew's that Canon Smith, the vicar of St Bartholomew's from 1871 to 1905, was president of the **Pembroke Ping-Pong Club** and around the 1930s there was a **Table Tennis Club** in that parish.[63] The **Table Tennis Club of St Stephen Parish** is mentioned in the history of St Stephen's Parish, but there is no indication of the years during which it flourished or where the club members played, though it is likely that they used the parochial hall.[64]

ESB Sportsco Table Tennis Club was established in 1979 in the Sportsco Centre in South Lotts Road, Ringsend. The club has a wide range of players of all different standards, nationalities and ages. It is affiliated to the Irish Table Tennis Association (ITTA) and plays in the Leinster Table Tennis League. They play every Monday and Wednesday evening. Wednesday night is the main club night and Monday night is used for home-league matches and training.

Squash

Old Belvedere Squash Racquets Club in Anglesea Road, Donnybrook, with the same address as Old Belvedere RFC, is the only squash club in the area, though Sportsco in Ringsend and David Lloyd Riverview, just at the border between Donnybrook, Dublin 4 and Clonskeagh, Dublin 14, have squash courts. Old Belvedere Squash Club shares the clubhouse with the rugby club.

Not too far outside the area in the former Rathmines and Rathgar Township is Fitzwilliam Lawn Tennis Club, which has a squash section as well.

Veterans' Handicap Semi-Final, 6 January 2012.
(Courtesy of Old Belvedere Squash Racquets Club)

Other
Ball Sports

Bowling

There are currently three lawn bowling clubs in this area, but only two venues as Bank of Ireland Bowling Club uses the green of Railway Union Bowling Club.

Railway Union Bowling Club, founded like other Railway Union Clubs in 1904, is the second-oldest bowling club in Dublin after Kenilworth Bowls Club, which was founded in 1892. Their bowling green is the oldest bowling

Railway Union Bowling. (Courtesy of Railway Union CC)

green still in use in Ireland. Originally it consisted of only three rinks. In 1932 a fourth rink was added in anticipation of the club's promotion to senior ranks; 1976 saw an extension to five rinks and in 2002, when the club was granted more land, a sixth rink was added. Railway Union Bowling Club originally only had men as members, but since 1975 it has also been open to women.

In 1927 the club was a founder member of the 'Irish Free State Bowling League', which was to become the Bowling League of Ireland (BLI). Members of Railway Bowling Club have been presidents of the Bowling League of Ireland (BLI) and the Ladies BLI.

Bank of Ireland Bowling Club plays in the same league as Railway Union but is much younger. It was founded in 1979 in Knockrabo and started in the former Gas Company Sports Grounds, which had been taken over by Bank of Ireland. When this property was sold in the late 1990s, the club arranged to move in 2000 to the Railway Union Grounds. They have their own pavilion, but share the bowling green with Railway Union Bowling Club.

Herbert Park Bowling Club is over sixty years old now and has four men's and two ladies' teams, as well as two teams in the Winter League. They take their name from Herbert Park where they use the all-weather bowling green.

IGB Bowls Club was the bowling club of the Irish Glass Bottle Company, which was in Irishtown. The site of the club, however, was in Goatstown, Dublin 14. The club was affiliated to the BLI in 1993, but due to the closure of the Irish Glass Bottle Company and the sale of their sports grounds they resigned from BLI in 2003.

Croquet

Croquet lawns in the area are mentioned more often than croquet clubs. Henry W.D. Dunlop laid out two croquet lawns in Lansdowne Road and founded **Lansdowne Croquet Club**, which hosted the Irish Croquet Championship in 1875. The championship was not a success as far as attendance was concerned and the croquet club obviously did not do better than the cricket club Dunlop had founded. Some lawn tennis clubs had croquet lawns as well, e.g. the Percy Lawn Tennis Club.

Herbert Park Croquet Club was started in 1987 on the initiative of the Croquet Association of Ireland, which itself was formed in 1985. The club currently has two full-sized lawns and about forty-five members who play association croquet and/or golf croquet. Several of their past and present members have played for Irish teams in international matches, although none had or has a world ranking (in Association Croquet) in the top 200.

In 2007 the Women's World Golf Croquet Championship came to Dublin and matches were played at Herbert Park, as well as at Carrickmines Croquet and Tennis Club.

Golf

Elm Park Golf Club was founded 1924 and is the only golf club in Dublin 4. The club purchased Elm Park House and some of its grounds in 1924 and a nine-hole golf course was opened 1925. Before 1924 the site was owned by the ffrench family. The Right Hon. Sir Thomas ffrench, 4th Baron ffrench,[65] moved into Elm Park House in the early 1870s. After his death in 1892 and the death of his widow Lady Mary Ann ffrench in 1906, the house was unoccupied until a member of another branch of the same family, Field Marshal John Denton French, Viscount French (later Earl of Ypres), Commander-in-Chief of Home Forces in 1916 and Lord Lieutenant in 1918, commandeered it in 1916 for the Irish Command Grenade School. Outlines of the trenches used in grenade training are still visible on sections of the course. Some of the grounds were sold in 1934 to the Sisters of Charity for the proposed St Vincent's Hospital. In 1936 Nutley House was leased back from them and tennis courts were opened in addition to the nine-hole golf course. In 1941 the golf course was extended to eighteen holes on the old Elm Park ground but that had to be given back in 1956 and the club had to revert to a nine-hole course. The present eighteen-hole course was opened in September 1960 following the purchase of the adjoining Bloomfield Estate. Samuel Lewis mentions both Elm Park and Bloomfield in 1837 in the Merrion section of his *Topographical Dictionary of Ireland* and Nutley House in the Donnybrook section.[66]

Nutley House has a beautiful garden behind which the golf course stretches to the south and east.

Riding, Driving, Cycling and Running

Horse Sports

When riding is mentioned in this area, the RDS Horse Show comes to mind immediately. This show has been held since 1864, first on Leinster Lawn and, since 1881, in the Ballsbridge grounds. It was here in Ballsbridge that the first continuous 'leaping' course was introduced at the show. International Competitions became part of the show in 1926 when the Nations' Cup for the Aga Khan Challenge trophy was held for the first time. Until 1949 the Nations' Cup teams had to consist of military officers. The first timed jumping competition was held in 1938. In 1951 an electric clock was installed and a time factor became part of most competitions. The Dublin Horse Show is Ireland's largest equestrian event and one of the largest events held on the island. The show has one of the largest annual prize pools for International Show Jumping in the world.

Apart from the Horse Show, riders can sometimes be seen exercising their horses on Sandymount and Merrion Strand.

Some centuries before the Horse Show, references to carriage racing are found in old newspapers. On 15 May 1665, *The Intelligencer* reported:

We have here upon the Strand several races; but the most remarkable was by the Ringsend coaches, (Which is an odde kind of carre, and generally used in the countrye.) There was a matter of twenty-five of them, and his Excellency the Lord Deputy (Thomas Earl of Ossory) bestowed a piece of plate upon him that won the race, and the second, third and

Titled: 'Well over' – A Military Contest. (Photo: Frank O'Brien)

Galloping on Merrion Strand.

fourth were rewarded with money. It is a new institution and likely to become an annual custom; for the humour of it gives much satisfaction, there being at least five thousand spectators.[67]

It is not known if the races did become an annual event, but more than one hundred years later another newspaper report indicates that racing still happened on the strand at the end of the eighteenth century:

The Rt. Honbl. the Lord Mayor (Aldmn. George Reynolds) and sheriffs (M/s Blen. Grove and Anthony Perriers) went to Ringsend and took down the tents and likewise put a stop to horse racing intended to be there during the week.[68]

Even without races, a pony and trap occasionally appears on Sandymount Strand.

Pony and trap on Sandymount Strand.

Cycling

Cycling became fashionable in the last quarter of the nineteenth century. In the 1880s, prices for the 'Ordinary', known as a 'Penny-Farthing', as well as the 'Safety Bike', which resembles a modern bike, ranged between £12 and £20 (the annual income of a primary school teacher at that time was £16). Cycling was soon adopted by the RIC (Royal Irish Constabulary) and also by the clergy, although some members of the hierarchy wondered if cycling was appropriate for people in holy orders. At a meeting of Catholic bishops at Maynooth, this was one of the points planned for discussion. The point was dropped when William J. Walsh, Archbishop of Dublin and Primate of Ireland, arrived in Maynooth, riding from his palace in Dublin – on his bike.[69]

Cycling clubs sprang up everywhere and soon there were cycling competitions and races. H.W.D. Dunlop's Irish Champion Athletic Club originally had a cycling section as well. Dublin 4 has seen many cycling events: for instance, bicycle polo matches in 1890. A cycling track was built in the RDS Grounds in 1888 and afterwards most Irish championship races were held there or in the Phoenix Park.[70]

The **Irish Champion Bicycling Club** was founded in 1875 and had an arrangement with H.W.D. Dunlop that allowed them to use the track in Lansdowne Road. This worked until the 1880s, when the track fell into disrepair and the club moved from Lansdowne Road to the RDS. The Irish Champion Bicycling Club was an all-Ireland club and organised the All-Ireland Cycling Championship in 1877 in Lansdowne Road in tandem with the championship of the Irish Champion Athletic Club. In 1884 the Irish Champion Bicycling Club was replaced by the Irish Cycling Association, which competed with the GAA as far as cycling was concerned. By 1910 the Irish Cycling Association had folded.

Trinity College students held races in College Park, but participated at other locations as well. Oliver St John Gogerty took part in such races during his student days. Ulick O'Connor mentions in his biography of the wit, poet and, later, famous surgeon and senator, that the *Freeman's Journal* reported on Gogarty winning the double, half-mile and the two-mile handicap there.

But cycling was not only races or polo matches. Brian Griffin refers to *Irish Cyclist Magazine*, which at some time mentions that the Sandymount area was in June 1887 swarming with cyclists, including a great number of the 'fair sex'.

The same author also mentions that the **Sandymount Cycling Club** and the **Pembroke Cycling Club**, which were both established in early summer 1887, were among the few clubs that accepted male and female members from the beginning. At that time, ladies usually rode tricycles as the lady's safety bicycle was only slowly coming onto the market and the 'Ordinary' would have been impossible to ride for a lady in a long dress. According to Griffin, the president of Pembroke Cycling Club in 1890 was Sir Robert William Jackson, CB, MD, Deputy Surgeon-General. Sir Robert lived in Newgrove Avenue in Sandymount and died there on 13 May 1921, aged 93.[71]

Judging from reports on demand and sales, women's bicycles replaced most of the tricycles in the mid-1890s. Cycling clubs met frequently on social outings, but there were always members training for races (for ordinary bicycles, safety bicycles and tricycles) as well as bicycle polo matches.

In 1890 two of the sons of Harvey du Cros Sr, Arthur and Harvey Jr, as well as Richard J. Mecredy, were part of the Irish cycling team that won races on English tracks, using pneumatic tyres from the factory of Harvey Sr. Mecredy (1861–1924) was the editor of *Irish Cycling Magazine* and the inventor of bicycle polo in the sense that he wrote the rules for it in 1891. He lived in Bray but practised for his racing in Ballsbridge. His son Ralph Jack Richard Mecredy (1888–1968), who in 1911 lived in Gilford Road, Sandymount, was also a noted cyclist and participated in the 1912 Olympics in Stockholm.

Bicycle polo was an important sport at the turn of the twentieth century and for some time later. After the Second World War, it more or less disappeared in Ireland and Britain, but at the turn of the millennium it re-appeared. Today Ireland's only bicycle polo club is based in the Phoenix Park.

In the 1950s, bicycle races were still held in this area. As there were no tarmacadamed tracks in Ireland then, races were held on grass, as in the Lansdowne Road Stadium in 1951. That was when Henry Whelan, who was there for another event, was asked to stand in for an English cyclist who had not turned up. He accepted the challenge and raced the 1,000m against other famous Irish cyclists like Jim McQuaid, Jack Ryan and Noel Tully. Not only did he make the final, he actually won the event in a tight sprint.[72]

Athletics

In the mid- and late nineteenth century, when football had not yet become popular on a wide scale, the national sport in Ireland was track and field athletics. Every town and village had its meetings and most were highly successful. Irish athletes led the world at that time and some track and field events were invented in Ireland, like the hop, step and jump, now called triple jump, and also the hammer throw. The year 1857 saw the first 440-yard hurdle race in Trinity College Park, using fifteen hurdles rather than the modern ten. Four years later, in 1860, the weight for the shot still used today – 16lbs – was established in Trinity College.[73]

The **Irish Champion Athletic Club** (ICAC), initially named 'Royal Irish Athletic Club', was founded by Henry W.D. Dunlop in 1872, originally in Trinity College Park, but it had to move from there very shortly afterwards. It got its own grounds during its first year of existence in what later became the Lansdowne Road Stadium (now Aviva Stadium). The athletic club founded by Dunlop did not survive long, however. In 1876 Dunlop proposed turning the club into a company to finance more expansion on Lansdowne Road. This led to a split and in the summer of 1880 the tenancy of Lansdowne Road was passed from the ICAC to Lansdowne Football Club and in December 1880 the Irish Champions Athletic Club was dissolved.[74] Despite the fact that it was so short-lived, the ICAC introduced the first ideas to bring an orderly management to Irish amateur athletics.[75]

Crusaders Athletic Club is the only athletics club in this area today. The club was founded in 1942 and is based in Irishtown Stadium. Crusaders was the first club to cater for female members in athletics, opening a women's section in 1947, a move that was vigorously but unsuccessfully opposed by Archbishop John Charles McQuaid of Dublin. Mary Tracey-Purcell, national-record holder in 800m, 1,500m and 3,000m in the 1970s, was a member of Crusaders AC. The club concentrates on running, including road running, cross-country running and mountain running, apart from track and field events.

The most famous member of Crusaders was Ronnie Delany, gold-medal winner in the Melbourne Olympics in 1956. Fifty years after that event, An Post honoured him with a commemorative stamp.

Ray Hynes in the leading group
of the men's 3,000m race,
8 May 2010.
(Courtesy of Crusaders AC)

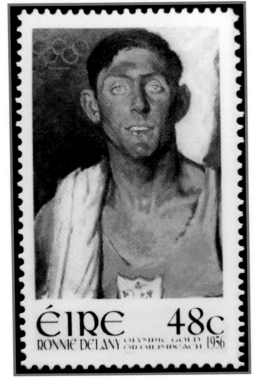

Ronnie Delany commemorative
stamp (2006). (Reproduction by
kind permission of An Post ©)

Combat Sports

Combat sports developed from single combat fights and duels. Fights originally lasted until one fighter was dead or had to beg for his life. Duels could also lead to the death of one of the participants. Today the matches are different.

Boxing

Information on the **Sandymount Boxing Club** is hard to find and even its exact location is difficult to establish. *A Social and Natural History of Sandymount Irishtown Ringsend* states, 'The boxing club was on the right of Church Avenue'.[76] This would place the club either in Sandymount or in Irishtown. A website concerned with rowing includes the information that the premises of the Dolphin's Rowing Club at the mouth of the Dodder were sold to the Sandymount Boxing Club in 1941,[77] which would put the club into Ringsend, and another website indicates that Sandymount Boxing Club was 'off Pearse Street',[78] which would place it in Dublin 2. No information at all could be found about when it was founded or how long it existed. It seems to be established that the club was founded in the Sandymount/Irishtown area but soon started to move nearer and nearer the city centre.

The genealogy of the Murphy family gives information about some club members.[79] William Boxing Murphy – the middle name distinguished him from his father William Craneman Murphy, though the son was a crane driver by profession as well – born in around 1910 in Thomas Street, Ringsend, was the trainer for Sandymount Amateur Boxing Club from 1930 to 1960. His son Marty Murphy boxed in Sandymount Boxing Club, as did his nephews (and Marty's cousins) John Butcher Murphy and Thomas Butcher Murphy, who were active between 1940 and 1955. Two other members of Sandymount Boxing Club, the brothers Andrew (Ando) Reddy (b. 1933) and his older brother Thomas (Tommy) Reddy, were members of the Irish Boxing Team in the 1952 Helsinki Olympics and Ando also participated in the 1960 Olympics in Rome. He retired from boxing in 1962.

Fencing

Salle d'Armes Duffy, the oldest fencing school in modern Ireland, was founded by Patrick Joseph Duffy in 1952. According to his widow Shirley Duffy (*née* Armstrong), Paddy Duffy had been a member of St Vincent's GAA Club in Marino, Dublin 3, during his young years. He joined the Irish Army in July 1940 as 2nd lieutenant and it was there that he first encountered fencing. The Curragh Military Fencing Club was instructed by French masters and under them Duffy became outstanding in this sport. He resigned from the

From an advertisement for Salle d'Armes Duffy. (Courtesy of Shirley Duffy)

army in 1946 with glowing recommendations. From 1947 to 1952, he was Irish All Weapons Champion and represented Ireland in the Olympic Games 1948 (London) and 1952 (Helsinki). After the Helsinki Games, he turned professional, qualified as a Maître d'Armes and became a member of the German, as well as the French, Academy of Arms. Duffy ran training courses – including for the 1959/60 Finnish Olympic fencing team, among others. He was a member of the International and the Irish Academy of Arms. He was known as 'the Prof' as the title 'Maître' was anglicised into 'Professor'.

Prof. Duffy, ADFD, AAI, AAF,[80] founded Salle d'Armes Duffy in 1952. At first he gave classes in rented rooms, including at some stage a room rented from Merrion Cricket Club. He and his wife Shirley participated in many competitions not only in Ireland, but also in the UK and on the Continent. He taught in several schools, of which St Conleth's is the only one that still teaches the sport.

In 1962 Patrick Duffy acquired the former parochial hall of St John the Evangelist on the border between Sandymount and Merrion, which he rebuilt as a Salle d'Armes with a fencing hall on the ground floor and a lounge, shower and changing rooms in the first floor. It became the centre of fencing for Ireland and many of its fencers participated in Olympic Games.

Patrick J. Duffy. (Courtesy of Shirley Duffy)

Salle d'Armes Duffy.

After his death in 1987, his widow Shirley Duffy kept Salle d'Armes Duffy going for nearly another twenty years. She competed in the 1960 Olympic Games (Rome) and was the first Irishwoman to qualify as a Maître d'Armes. Like her husband, she especially enjoyed teaching young people, starting with children of 7 years of age. She is Président d'Honneur of the Irish Academy of Armes.

Salle Dublin was founded in 2005 by Maître David Couper and Maître Fionbarr Farrell. They had both been working in Salle d'Armes Duffy, Farrell as fencing master and Couper as Maître Assistant. Fionbarr Farrell fenced for Ireland at the World Championships between 1965 and 1978 and won most Irish titles several times. In 1968 he represented Ireland at the Olympic Games in Mexico City and was National Foil Champion in 1992/3. David Couper was the founding vice president of the Modern Pentathlon Association of Ireland (MPAI) and was formerly the MPAI fencing coach. They see it as their mission to take Irish fencing to another level of excellence and place a strong emphasis on individual development and personal lessons. Salle Dublin practises in Liffey Trust Studios and St Conleth's College Gym, Clyde Road, Ballsbridge.

Fencing in Salle d'Armes Duffy in the 1960s. (Courtesy of Shirley Duffy)

Trophies and memorabilia in the lounge of Salle d'Armes Duffy.
(With kind permission of Shirley Duffy)

Pembroke Fencing Club was founded in 2001. It is based in St Conleth's College, Clyde Road. Their coach, Maitre d'Armes Olga Velma, specialises in developing the sport for schoolchildren and students. They have competed in Ireland and abroad, including in the prestigious 2011 Marathon Foil tournament in Paris. They have a dedicated junior section, but the club says that fencing is a sport for men and women of all ages and abilities, and one doesn't have to be incredibly fit to be a competent fencer.[81]

Martial Arts

Taekwon-Do Sandymount is in existence since over twenty years with Richie Cullen as instructor who now is 3rd Dan Black Belt. The club has around fifteen members, some of which have achieved Black Belt status. Their practice times are Thursday and Friday 7–8 p.m. in the Star of the Sea School in Sandymount.

Taekwon-Do is a Korean art of self-defence founded in 1955 and introduced to Ireland in 1968. Taekwon-Do means 'the way of the foot and the fist'. It is based on traditional Korean Martial Arts and was developed using the principles of modern science.

Irishtown Karate Club was founded in 2003. Karate originated in Okinawa, Japan, with roots going back into the fourteenth century. During the last 400 years, it has developed into one of the best forms of self-defence. The World Traditional Karate Organization (WTKO) was founded in 2001 and WTKO (Ireland), to which Irishtown Karate Club is affiliated, was set up in 2014. The Hombu Dojo (Headquarter Club) is in Ranelagh.

Scott Langley, 6th Dan, is their chief instructor. Scott also taught the Irishtown Club when it started in 2003. He has a long career in karate and is one of only five non-Japanese who graduated from the instructor's course of the Japan Karate Shotorenmei World Headquarters in Tokyo during the fifty-five years of that institution's existence. He is now teaching in Ranelagh. The Irishtown club today is taught by Ross Steward, 2nd Dan, who had previously been coaching the Scotland squad at the WUKF (World Union of Karate Federations) European Championships.

Irishtown Karate Club classes are on Wednesdays in Irishtown Stadium.

Water Sports

Swimming and Water Polo

Peter Somerville-Large states that in the eighteenth century swimming was fashionable, especially after a Dubliner managed to swim from Dunleary (now Dún Laoghaire) to Howth in 1759.[82]

A. Peter confirms this when writing about the last decades of the eighteenth century, in which, according to her, it was said that 'the ladies of Dublin were remarkable for their good dancing and the men for their swimming'.[83]

It took another hundred years and more for this interest in swimming to be organised into a club.

Half Moon Swimming Club was founded in 1898 at (actually on) the Great South Wall in Dublin. It was known originally as 'The Poolbeg Bathers Association'. Later, when members began to enter swimming competitions, the name was changed to Half Moon Swimming Club.

The clubhouse sits approximately halfway along the South Wall, near the area known as Poolbeg, which for centuries served as an anchoring place for Dublin as it did not fall dry at low tide. Later, a small harbour was built at the South Wall and afterwards a fort with a gun battery was erected to protect the entrance to the port. The gun turret was mounted in a half-moon shape, hence the name of the club. Club members refer to their clubhouse as 'the Wall', 'the Poolbeg', 'the Battery' or 'the Half Moon'.

Three members – Shane Moraghan (1999), Pat Manning (1999) and Pat Nash (2001) – have completed solo English Channel swims, with Shane

Half Moon Swimming Club on the South Wall, looking east.

Preparing to get in. (Courtesy of Half Moon Swimming Club)

Moraghan managing this feat in the short time of 10 hour 23 minutes. Since 1946 club members have been winners of the Liffey Swim fifteen times and the Harbour Swim ten times.

Half Moon Swimming Club has a large water polo section, which is one of the most successful water polo clubs in Ireland with teams in all competitions from junior (under-16) through to senior level, including ladies. The men's team won the Irish Senior Cup (the premier national senior event) in 2014 for the twenty-second time. The ladies' team won the title in 2011 for the ninth time.

Several of their men's and ladies' members were called into the Irish National Water Polo team. Their water polo coach is also the coach for the national team. Water polo training and indoor swimming takes place at the National Aquatic Centre while open-sea swimming continues at the Half Moon clubhouse.

ESB Swimming Club has existed for over fifty-five years now. Since 1979 they have shared facilities with other sports in the ESB Sports Centre (Sportsco) in South Lotts Road in Ringsend. ESB Swimming Club activities include teaching classes for beginners as well as coaching swimmers for competitions. The club competes successfully at all major swimming galas in Ireland, including the National Championship, to which it generally brings a fifteen-strong team. In 2014 their members included an individual Irish record holder and an Irish record-holding relay team.[84]

Marian Water Polo Club is an amateur sports team that was founded in June 1967 in Marian College, Sandymount. Drawing players from the school and alumni, the club became rather successful in Irish water polo, winning leagues and cups.

Rowing

Rowing was well represented in Ringsend even before the nineteenth century; however, it was not a sport then but a hard and dangerous way to earn a living. Hobblers – professional boatmen – rowed out in all weathers to pilot schooners into the harbour. The crew of the boat that reached the schooner first won the contract, so there was very strong competition. Hobbling ceased in Dublin in 1936, but boats in the design of hobblers' boats are still made.

East Coast skiff.

They are 'traditional boats of the Ringsend design', made of wood, wider than racing rowing boats and, like in old hobbling times, laid out for four rowers – but they do not have provisions for sails any more.

Hobbling was a hard life. Gerry Brannocks, historian of Ringsend's East Coast Rowing Clubs and member of Stella Maris Rowing Club for over sixty years, is the son-in-law of one of the last Dublin hobblers. According to Gerry, this hobbler had a friend near Wexford who sent him a telegram whenever he knew of a schooner travelling towards Dublin. The Dublin hobbler then had to work out the probable time of arrival of that schooner, taking into account wind strength and direction, weather conditions and tides, to know when to go out with his team to meet the schooner, but still he might have been beaten by a team going out from Dún Laoghaire.

Rowing as a sport developed independently, also in Ringsend. In 1836 university men from Trinity College formed the **Pembroke Club**, which was 'primarily concerned with the rowing of small boats at Ringsend', although they played other sports as well.[85] R.M. Peter, for instance, mentions a football match between the Pembroke Club and Wanderers FC in Clyde Road, played on 11 October 1879, which Wanderers won by two goals and two tries.[86] In 1847 it was decided to restrict membership to those with ties to Trinity College. At the same time, they amalgamated with the **University Rowing Club** to become the Dublin University Rowing Club.[87] At the Malahide Regatta of 1858, they were referred to as Dublin University Club.[88] In 1868

Rowing in Ringsend in the early twentieth century.

Thom's Directory mentions 'University Rowing Club – William Colquhoun, keeper' in Thorncastle Street in Ringsend. Other entries for the same street in that directory – in alphabetical order and without further specification – read 'Dublin Rowing Club – John Hogan, esq. honorary sec.; John Coughlin, store-keeper', 'Fitzwilliam Rowing Club', 'Liffey Rowing Club' and 'Neptune Rowing Club – John Barnes store-keeper'. Fitzwilliam Rowing Club and Liffey Rowing Club do not exist anymore.

Dublin University Boat Club split from the Dublin University Rowing Club in 1881, but both clubs amalgamated again in 1898. In the same year, they moved from Ringsend to Islandbridge as the waters at Ringsend were too rough, as well as being full of debris. They were the first of the rowing clubs to make the move to the much more pleasant settings on the Liffey in what was then the countryside west of Dublin. In due course, more clubs would follow them. Bram Stoker was a member of Dublin University Boat Club.[89] **Neptune Rowing Club** exists still, but gives 1908 as its foundation date. Like many others, they are situated in Islandbridge. Brendan O'Donoghue, their honorary secretary, is not sure if the name is a coincidence or if the older club dissolved and some former members then founded the new club.

Dublin Rowing Club was founded in 1906 in Chapelizod and stayed in exist-ence until at least 1942. As in the case of Neptune Rowing Club, there might have been an earlier version of the club in Ringsend as a history of Dublin Rowing Club says of the year 1908 that from then on rowing was split between the clubs that remained in Ringsend, i.e. the Commercial Rowing Club and the Dolphin Rowing Club and the clubs that had moved to Islandbridge.[90]

According to the same source, Dublin Rowing Club got into difficulties in 1942 and, after a planned merger with Commercial Rowing Club was blocked by the latter, they finally closed in the summer of 1942. Their estate was taken over by Commercial Rowing Club, which moved from Ringsend to Islandbridge in the same year.

Commercial Rowing Club was founded in 1856 and is the second-oldest rowing club in the country. At that time, all non-university clubs were called 'commercial'. The original membership was drawn from the commercial heart of Dublin: bankers, tailors and shopkeepers of Henry Street and Grafton Street. A good number of the original members were employees of Clery's, which had been founded just three years earlier. Their boathouse was located in Ringsend. The traditional source of membership lasted right up until the 1950s, after which it started to change. Commercial was one of the clubs that formed the short-lived Amateur Rowing Association in the early 1880s. The club moved upstream to Islandbridge in 1942 to take over the premises of Dublin Rowing Club, which had become insolvent.

The OS map of 1907 shows Commercial Rowing Club and Dolphin Rowing Club on the right bank of the Dodder shortly before the locks of the Grand Canal Dock open into it further down stream and the 1911 census has them in Commercial Court and Thorncastle Place respectively. For the 1940s, it is said that Dolphin Rowing Club and Commercial Rowing Club were only shadows of what they had been in 1914.[91]

Dolphin Rowing Club closed shortly after Dublin Rowing Club in 1942.

University College Dublin Rowing Club, founded in 1917, was at first a tenant of the Commercial Rowing Club in Ringsend before they moved in with Dolphin Rowing Club in 1919 because this club had more boats and fewer rowers. In 1926 they were renamed **University College Dublin Boat Club (UCDBC)** and in 1928 they moved to Islandbridge where they became tenants of Dublin Rowing Club. In 1932 they were able to purchase their own boathouse. At the London Olympics in 1948, the Ireland VIII included six members of UCDBC and in the following years many members competed in international regattas.

The reason why rowing clubs moved from Ringsend to Islandbridge is described by UCDBC in similar words to those that were used by Dublin University Boat Club. They added that the neighbourhood in Ringsend was shabby, with the Dodder carrying dead animals, old beds and bicycles that occasionally got stuck in the mud and appeared at low tide. On top of everything else, a glue factory nearby filled the neighbourhood with an awful, sickly smell.[92]

The two rowing clubs that are still resident in Ringsend belong to the East Coast Rowing Council of the Irish Coastal Rowing Association as distinct from the Irish Amateur Rowing Union, which caters for rowing on inland waterways.

Stella Maris Rowing Club is a descendant of Cambridge Athletic Club, which was founded in 1931 and established in 1932. Its members were seafarers and fishermen, unsurprisingly, considering its location in Ringsend. Originally the club was mainly a football team which, though a tough lot, had the nickname 'The Chickens'. The reason for this nickname

Members of Cambridge Athletic Club, *c.* 1932. (Courtesy of David Doyle)

is not known. The rowing club started some years later, around 1936, probably at the mouth of the Dodder. They have now moved to the shore of the Liffey, where they still have regattas.

According to Gerry Brannocks, the two Ringsend rowing clubs stem from the same root. In 1933 the only rowing boat in Ringsend was the one of the confraternity men of the parish of St Patrick's.

Different crews, including one of the Cambridge Athletic Club, used that single boat and this frequently led to disagreements. Around 1936 the Cambridge men opted out and acquired a boat for themselves. From 1936 on, there were two rowing clubs in Ringsend: St Patrick's (after the Ringsend parish), established as a club in 1936, and Cambridge Stella Maris (taking the name from the neighbouring Sandymount parish), established shortly after. This led to an everlasting discussion between the two clubs about their age. Cambridge Athletic Club, the parent of Stella Maris Rowing Club, is the older club, but St Patrick's was the first club established as a rowing club.

Stella Maris Rowing Club had to give up some of their land when the East Link Bridge was built and now have a new clubhouse on Poolbeg Street. They have men's, women's and mixed teams, as well as teams for boys and girls, under-14 and under-12.

A mixed regatta on the Liffey in the Docklands.
(Courtesy of David Doyle, second from left in the near boat)

Club house, Stella Maris Rowing Club, Ringsend.

Some time ago, the Dublin Docklands Development Authority (DDDA) tried to combine the two clubs into a single 'DDDA Rowing Club', but nothing came of this proposal. There are still two rowing clubs in Ringsend.

St Patrick's Rowing Club was the first skiff rowing club formed in the parish of Ringsend. Although they were established in 1936, they had owned and crewed a boat since 1933 as confraternity men of St Patrick's parish. Their clubhouse is on York Road, just at the end of Thorncastle Street, beside the mouth of the Dodder. They own the site and the clubhouse has been there since 1985, but they have built extensions to it.

On the Liffey (before the Samuel-Beckett-Bridge was built). (Courtesy of Philip Murphy)

Club house, St Patrick's Rowing Club, Ringsend.

A crew of St Patrick's Rowing Club. (Courtesy of Philip Murphy)

St Pat's has rowing teams of all ages and welcomes anyone who wishes to become involved. The club has developed significantly over the past ten years. St Pat's hosts an annual regatta every June which attracts a number of rowing clubs from the east coast of Ireland.

East coast rowers are traditional people and they prefer their wood-built clinker skiffs. For all-Ireland regattas, they have to use fibreglass boats, but as their historian Philip Murphy says, 'If God had meant us to row in fibreglass boats, he would have created fibreglass trees.'

Yachting

Poolbeg Yacht and Boat Club, founded in 1976, had a trawler as their first clubhouse, but this sank and only bits of it could be retrieved. They finally built a new clubhouse in 1984 right beside the new Stella Maris clubhouse.

Clubhouse,
Poolbeg Yacht and
Boat Club, Ringsend.

Sailing near the South Wall. (Courtesy of Poolbeg Yacht and Boat Club)

Apart from the new clubhouse, they have also developed a state-of-the-art, 100-berth marina facility. As the marina is on the Liffey side of Ringsend, they have to pass the South Wall to sail into the open waters of Dublin Bay.

Other water sports

Windsurfing, especially kite-surfing, is well established in Dublin Bay and surfers are frequently seen in the area, south of the South Wall, as well as on Sandymount and Merrion Strand. There are no clubs in Dublin 4; the nearest one is Dublin University Windsurfing Club in Dublin 2, which, however, trains in Malahide.

During recent decades, the Grand Canal Basin has been developed for water sports. When the old Aran Island ferry *Naomh Éanna* was still moored at Charlotte Dock, a windsurfing school had its home on-board. This school is still situated at Charlotte Dock, teaching windsurfing, paddleboarding and kayaking in the Grand Canal Basin. Later, another school beside the windsurfers introduced Ireland's first cable wakeboard park.

Windsurfer at Merrion Strand.

Kayakers at Ballsbridge Weir in the Dodder.

Kayaking clubs are based upriver from Dublin City, apart from the **East Coast Sea Kayaking Club**, which has existed since 2002. They have around eighty members and cover the whole Irish east coast. They do not have a fixed address, though their twice-weekly meetings are mostly held in or around the Dublin area. Kayaks can be seen in Dublin 4 occasionally: for instance, when two enterprising young men try to paddle up the Dodder past the Ballsbridge weir, the nearest one to the sea.

Sport Venues

According to Clanna Gael-Fontenoy, the first Dublin Hurling and Football Championship was held in Elm Park in 1887. The GAA used grounds loaned by Lord ffrench, which were regarded as very suitable for hurling and football matches. In 1913 the GAA shortlisted two sites as suitable for a national GAA stadium: one at Elm Park, Dublin 4, the other at Jones's Road, Dublin 3. At a meeting on 15 September 1913, it was proposed to buy Elm Park, but although the proposal was seconded, it was not voted upon. At a subsequent meeting three weeks later, a vote gave Elm Park seven votes and Jones's Road eight.

As all rugby, cricket, hockey and tennis clubs, the GAA club and two of the three bowls clubs in Dublin 4 have their own sports grounds, the following describes communal and private sport venues that are not particular to or owned by a club. Former venues that have disappeared are mentioned in the history of the clubs that used them.

Dublin City Council Grounds

Pembroke Urban Council and later Dublin Corporation, which on 1 January 2002 took the name Dublin City Council, provided sport venues in their public parks in Ringsend, Ballsbridge and Irishtown.

Ringsend Park
Ringsend Park was developed on land reclaimed from the sea between 1905 and 1908. The Earl of Pembroke, as landlord, offered it to Pembroke

A soccer pitch in Ringsend Park.

Urban Council. Since the summer of 1909, it has provided grounds for Gaelic football and soccer.[94] These grounds are used by a number of soccer clubs, as well as the GAA club Clanna Gael-Fontenoy.

Herbert Park

In 1903 the Earl of Pembroke granted the land for Herbert Park to Pembroke Urban Council, but as the area was first used for the International Exhibition of 1907, the public park was only created in 1911. The original design had included grounds for cricket, soccer, croquet and tennis. Pembroke Urban Council was incorporated into Dublin in 1930 and Dublin Corporation took over the administration of Herbert Park in 1932. At that stage, the park had neither a cricket ground nor a croquet lawn. In 1944 the Corporation laid out the first municipal bowling green of modern times in Dublin there.[95] The OS map of 1944 shows tennis courts beside the bowling green and a football pitch at the southern end of the park.[96] The croquet lawn was laid down later.

Bowling green, Herbert Park.

Croquet green, Herbert Park.

Irishtown Stadium

Irishtown Stadium provides a venue for a variety of sports. It is in public hands now, but it was built as a private venue. Its history is more complex than that of other Dublin City Council venues. The land on which it is built was reclaimed from the sea in the 1930s and owned by the Pembroke Estate. From December 1936, Dublin Corporation held an Indefeasible Licence in Perpetuity from the Earl of Pembroke for this land. In 1948 the Corporation renounced the licence and consented that the Earl of Pembroke lease the land to Shelbourne FC. The lease was granted in 1948 and signed by Shelbourne in November 1950. After five years of development, the stadium could finally be used. Shelbourne FC was persuaded to have a running track around the football pitch in the hope that athletic events could be held there. This track meant that spectators were kept further away from the pitch than they were used to.

Adverse climatic and financial conditions resulted in the stadium not being a success for Shelbourne FC. Frequent strong winds interfered with sport activities and the club's money had run out before decent facilities for spectators could be built. The first team of Shelbourne FC used the stadium only for the 1955/56 season. Until the 1970s, their youth teams played there; after that, it fell into decay.[97] In 1975 Dublin Corporation acquired two leases granted to Shelbourne FC in 1948 and 1959 and in 1976 the Corporation acquired the freehold.

Irishtown Stadium.

Memorial to Alan Young at Irishtown Stadium.

In 2002 the stadium was rebuilt and proper facilities were added by Dublin City Council. It is now used by Crusaders AC, Dundrum South Dublin AC, UCD AC and DU HAC (Dublin University Harriers and Athletic Club), as well as a number of soccer clubs. The Irishtown Karate Club uses it as well, as do some groups playing tag rugby or practising aerobics.

Irishtown Stadium has an eight-lane, 400m running track, an AstroTurf pitch, a grass soccer pitch, five '5-a-side' all-weather pitches, a fully equipped gym, an aerobics studio, meeting rooms and seven dressing rooms. Since August 2014, it has been undergoing reconstruction, which means that the running track as well as the infield throwing and jumping areas cannot be used until the work is finished.

At the edge of the stadium, there is a memorial for Alan Young, a gifted young soccer player who was twice capped for the National Irish Junior Team. He died tragically, aged 19, on 11 March 2007.

Shelbourne Park

Shelbourne Park is known as a greyhound-racing stadium. This, however, was not its original use. Like Irishtown Stadium, it was developed by Shelbourne FC, who leased the ground in 1913. Shelbourne FC won an Irish Cup in the Irish League there, five league titles and an FAI Cup in the League of Ireland in 1921. Shelbourne Park was the venue for two FAI Cup Final replays, in 1927 and 1929.

Shelbourne Park.

Greyhound races started in Shelbourne Park in 1927; the first race was held on 14 May. At the end of the 1940s, the lease for Shelbourne FC ran out. According to Shelbourne historian N. Chris Sands, the ground was then owned by Paddy O'Donoghue, the owner of O'Donoghue's Pub in Suffolk Street.[98] Other sources confirm the name Paddy O'Donoghue, but identify him as the head of the IRA in Manchester from 1919 to 1921, a friend of Michael Collins.[99] O'Donoghue offered to sell Shelbourne Park to the football club. Shelbourne FC decided not to take up the offer but to build its own stadium instead: Irishtown Stadium.

Speedway races were staged in Shelbourne Park from 1950 to 1954 and again in 1961. In 2005, Shelbourne Park saw a race between a Mazda MX-5 sports car and a greyhound. The car's time was 35.60 seconds; the greyhound managed the same distance in 31.98 seconds.[100]

Donnybrook Stadium

Donnybrook Stadium is sometimes referred to as Donnybrook Rugby Grounds. Locally it is often called 'Old Wesley' or 'Bective' after the two rugby clubs who use it. It is owned by the Leinster Branch of the Irish Rugby Football Union (IRFU). On the OS map of 1907, the area is still called 'Old Fair Green' without any sign of a sports ground. Bective Rangers FC moved there in around 1910.[101] A report of the annual general meeting of Old Wesley RFC in September 1919 says that they had arranged to become tenants of the Leinster Branch at the new Donnybrook grounds.[102]

Donnybrook Stadium from Donnybrook Road.

In 1977 the headquarters of the Leinster Branch of the IRFU moved from Westmoreland Street to Donnybrook.[103] The idea to develop the stadium further was first broached in the 1990s, but soon Leinster Rugby realised that the stand was too small and too old and the capacity of the stadium was not big enough considering the numbers of spectators it could accommodate as well as the matches the pitch could take. Leinster moved to the RDS Arena in 2007, at a time when the new stand in Donnybrook alongside Donnybrook Road was built. This stand was opened on 27 January 2008.

The year 2008 saw a Michael Bublé concert take place there. In 2012 the Global Ireland Football Tournament organised two American football matches in Donnybrook on 31 August 2012, the first between two American high school football teams: Jesuit (Dallas, Texas) v. Wilmette Loyola Academy (Wilmette, Illinois). Jesuit defeated Loyola 30–29, with a last-minute, game-winning field goal. According to a report of the *Chicago Tribune*, the match was not a particularly aesthetic way to acquaint the Irish with American football.[104]

The second match was John Carroll University (University Heights, Ohio) v. St Norbert College (De Pere, Wisconsin), which John Carroll University won 40:3. This marked the first time in twenty years an NCAA (National Collegiate Athletic Association) Division III regular season game was played in Europe.

In 2014 the pitch of Donnybrook Stadium was completely renewed.

Donnybrook Stadium in July 2014 with the pavilion of Old Wesley in the background.

Donnybrook Stadium in the first days of 2015 with the
pavilion of Bective Rangers in the background.

Just half a year later the renovations were finished and the stadium had
a new synthetic pitch.

Apart from Bective Rangers and Old Wesley, the grounds are used by
Ireland Wolfhounds (formerly Ireland A), the Ireland Women's National
Rugby Team, Amateur Internationals and Leinster A. As well as that, many
Leinster school rugby matches are played in Donnybrook Stadium.

RDS Arena

The RDS acquired grounds in Ballsbridge in 1879 and the first 'Ball's Bridge
Show' was held in April 1881. RDS shows included horse jumping from
the first Horse Show in the courtyard of Leinster House in 1868 and this
continued in Ballsbridge. The best-known event, the Aga Khan Trophy, was
first held in 1926.

From the beginning, the RDS Grounds were not only used for horse
sports. Cycling was one of the first other sports to avail of the grounds.

The drawing shows that this ground had a stand from its first years.
As St Mary's church in Donnybrook can be seen in the background, the view
is towards the south, so the first stand was where the Grand Stand is now.

RDS ground prepared for a bicycle race in 1886. (*Irish Cyclist*, 17 February 1886)

In athletics the Ballsbridge grounds of the RDS saw victories of the Irish champion runner T.P. Conneff from Clane, County Kildare. Conneff won the mile and half mile in the 'Caledonian Games and Sports' in Ballsbridge in June 1886 and in the same distances the Irish Championship one month later on 23 July. In August 1887, he ran the 'four-mile Marathon' against the then English and American champion E.C. Carter. Conneff had won a race against Carter in England and as an Irishman he was favoured by the Dublin audience. To the delight of 20,000 people, the biggest crowd watching an athletic race in Ireland to date, he won this race as well. His time of 19 minutes and 14.8 seconds was a new world record.

Conneff emigrated to the United States shortly afterwards, turned professional in 1896, enlisted in the US Army at the outbreak of the Spanish-American war in 1898, served in Cuba, Puerto Rico and the Philippines, and was drowned in Manila in 1912.[105]

Other sport events in the RDS:

Athletics: GAA National Athletic Championships in 1886.
Cycling: A number of cycling races in the 1880s and 1890s.
Soccer: Between September 1990 and April 1996, the RDS Arena was the home pitch for Shamrock Rovers Football Club.

On 19 February 1992, the arena played host to a match between the soccer teams of the Republic of Ireland and Wales.

The RDS Arena was host of the 1994 UEFA Under-16 Championships; the FAI Cup Finals in 2007 and 2008; and the 2008/09 UEFA Cup match between St Patrick's Athletic and Hertha Berlin. St Pat's also played Steaua Bucureşti in the arena on 27 August 2009 in the play-off round of the opening season of the Europa League.

The Republic of Ireland played two international friendlies on 25 and 28 May 2010 against Paraguay and Algeria.

Tennis: In 1983 the Ireland team played there in the World Group of the Davis Cup for the only time; the match against a United States team, including John McEnroe, was played in the RDS rather than the usual venue, Fitzwilliam Lawn Tennis Club, to accommodate crowds of 6,000 each day.

Wrestling: In 2005, the RDS hosted a WWE SmackDown event as part of the WWE Summerbash tour of Europe.

The RDS Arena has been upgraded several times during its existence. In 2015 it has two covered and two uncovered stands. The covered stands are the Anglesea Stand on the north side and the Grand Stand on the south

RDS Anglesea Road Stand during construction, c. 1930.

side of the arena. An advertisement in the RDS Bi-Centenary Souvenir shows the stand during construction.[106] It looks similar to the West Stand of Lansdowne Road, which was built more than fifty years later.

The old wooden stand on the south side of the RDS Arena was replaced by the modern Grand Stand in 2006. Two years later, this was roofed.

RDS Arena, Anglesea Stand, 2014.

RDS Arena, Grand Stand from Simmonscourt Road.

Seen from the back, the Grand Stand looks similar to the stand of Donnybrook Stadium, which was built at the same time.

Since 2005 the main tenant of the RDS Arena has been Leinster Rugby, who moved there from Donnybrook Stadium. At that time, the pitch was re-laid and floodlighting introduced. In 2014 the RDS and Leinster Rugby announced their plan to develop the arena further, increasing its capacity to 25,000. They estimate a building time of eighteen months and work is due to start in 2016.

Aviva Stadium

The oldest (according to foundation) and at the same time the newest (architecturally) sports venue in the area is the Aviva Stadium, which replaced the Lansdowne Road Stadium and was erected between 2007 and 2010.

The stadium is situated east of the railway in Beggarsbush townland. The location is at the border between Irishtown and Sandymount where Beggarsbush townland meets with Sandymount townland (south of the Dodder) and Ballsbridge townland (west of the railway line). One of the new entrances is situated in Ballsbridge, west of the railway.

Aviva Stadium west entrances, accessed from Ballsbridge.

Apart from sport events, the Aviva Stadium is used for big concerts, as was the old Lansdowne Road Stadium. The number of concerts per year is restricted out of consideration for the neighbours, who also benefit from the fact that the Aviva Stadium is better soundproofed than the Lansdowne Road Stadium was, which had open sides to the north and south.

History of the stadium

The history of the venue that now is called the Aviva Stadium begins with Henry Wallace Doveton Dunlop (1844–1930). Dunlop was an engineer who had studied at Dublin University. As a student, he was involved in athletics, participating and winning 'pedestrian races', a sport that now is called 'Walking'. He founded the 'Royal Irish Athletic Club' in 1872 in Trinity College. In its first meeting in March 1873, the club was renamed 'Irish Champion Athletic Club'. As the members of the club were not all students of Dublin University, the club had to leave the college grounds, prompting Dunlop to look for a suitable area elsewhere. After visiting various grounds in the Pembroke Urban District he finally leased a site situated between the railway, Lansdowne Road, the River Dodder and Havelock Square from the Pembroke Estate for sixty-nine years, at a ground rent of £60 per annum. Apart from the athletics club, Dunlop also founded a tennis club, an archery club, a cricket club, a croquet club and a rugby club.

Dunlop enclosed and levelled the ground, laid down a cinder running track for the athletes as well as a cricket pitch, a croquet green, three football pitches and facilities for archery and lawn tennis at the cost of £1,000. He called his stadium 'The Royal Park Stadium'. After it was formally opened on 23 May 1873, by the Earl of Spencer, Lord Lieutenant of Ireland, the stadium saw its first rugby match in 1876. This made it the oldest rugby stadium, with 130 years of uninterrupted use. The rugby club had been more an afterthought to keep the athletes active in winter but it became the most important of the clubs Dunlop had founded. When the Irish Champion Athletic Club went into decline, the rugby club took over the tenancy of Lansdowne Road in summer 1880. In December 1880, it was decided to dissolve the Irish Champion Athletic Club.

In 1904 Henry Sheppard, then treasurer of the Irish Rugby Football Union (IRFU), bought the lease from Dunlop and after Sheppard's early death in 1906 the IRFU acquired it from his mother in the same year for £200. The IRFU bought a new lease for fifty years for an annual rent of £50 and finally bought the freehold in 1974.[107]

The first pitch on which Lansdowne FC played from 1873 onwards was not ideal as H.W.D. Dunlop remembered at the end of his life:

> The ground they played on ran along Havelock Square, but it lay so low that one winter I paddled a canoe in about 18 inches of water through the two goals, while a few sheep stood on a little island in the middle![108]

He got the pitch level raised by two feet.

A report about the opening ceremony in 1873 mentions a grandstand on the site. In 1908 the IRFU built a covered stand alongside the railway and an uncovered stand in the north-west corner of the ground over the Lansdowne club pavilion. Around 1915 there was a box for the press where the East Stand was later erected.

A hundred years after the event, Arminta Wallace wrote about the 'Pals' in *The Irish Times* of Monday, 9 February 2015, stating that in 1915 Dublin was still a largely Unionist city. As F.H. Browning, then president of the Irish Rugby Football Union, appealed for recruits, 220 young Irishmen signed up in Lansdowne Road. They became D Company of the 7th Battalion, Royal Dublin Fusiliers.

'The Pals' in Lansdowne Road. In the back the first Press Box can be seen with St Matthew's church in the mist on the left, *c.* August 1914. (Courtesy of Gerard Siggins)

Many of the 'Pals' did not return; 239 of them departed from Lemnos late in July 1915, arriving in Suvla on the Gallipoli peninsula in early August. When they left Gallipoli in September 1915, there were only seventy-nine that had not been killed, wounded or captured. Lansdowne FC alone lost thirty-nine members in the First World War.

The first School Athletic Championship had been planned in Lansdowne Road Stadium for Saturday, 20 May 1916, but because of the Easter Rising this had to be postponed until 23 September. In 1922 these championships moved from Lansdowne Road to Croke Park.[109]

As well as the press box and stands, there were club pavilions. Dunlop writes in his memoirs in the 1920s about the Lansdowne rugby club pavilions:

> The first pavilion which stood on the present site was burned down. The second was at the N.E. corner opposite to it, and the third (on the present site again) was also burnt. The present pavilion is the club's fourth habitation. I hope that it also may be replaced by a more worthy structure before long.[110]

After the First World War, members of Lansdowne FC and Wanderers FC, both tenants of the Lansdowne Road Stadium, reclaimed enough land from the River Dodder to build two back pitches, which enabled the main pitch to be turned into the configuration that it held from then until the old stadium was pulled down. In 1927 the old East Stand was erected and a terrace was built under it.

The year 1948 was a special year for Irish rugby and for its home stadium, Lansdowne Road. Led by their captain Karl Mullen, a hooker from Old Belvedere RFC, they not only won the Triple Crown, they won the first Grand Slam ever for the Irish team. Karl Mullen was still alive and fit enough to watch Ireland win her next Grand Slam on 21 March 2009. He died a month later on 27 April 2009.

In 1954 the Upper West Stand was built, but in 1977 it was demolished to enable the building of the new West Stand, opened in 1978. The East Stand was replaced by the 'new' East Stand in 1983.

Despite the fact that Dalymount Park was the official soccer stadium, Lansdowne Road had hosted the occasional soccer match since 1898. From 1990 Dalymount Park was no longer considered adequate or big enough for international soccer matches, which from then on took place in Lansdowne Road.

The Old East Stand before the replacement in 1983. (Courtesy of Gerard Siggins)

Soccer in Lansdowne Road has caused some headaches, not for sport but for politics. Rugby has just one organisation for the whole island of Ireland, the Irish Rugby Football Union (IRFU). The Irish Football Association (IFA) for soccer was based in Belfast and a split occurred in 1921. Since then, there has been the IFA in Belfast for soccer in the six counties of the North and the Football Association of Ireland (FAI) in Dublin for soccer in the Republic of Ireland. FIFA (Fédération Internationale de Football Association) has accepted both associations as members, so now there are two international Irish soccer teams.

When in 1972 Louis Kilcoyne, then owner of Shamrock Rovers, wanted to organise a charity match between Brazil and Ireland, the Brazilians agreed under the condition that they could play against an all-Ireland team. The players from both sides of the border were thrilled with the idea of playing Brazil, but officials and politicians created difficulties. Politics was finally overcome by putting a team of five Northern Ireland players and six Republic of Ireland players into the jerseys of Shamrock Rovers and calling the team 'Shamrock Rovers XI' instead of 'Irish XI'. The only national flag flown and the only national anthem heard in Lansdowne Road Stadium on that day were the Brazilian ones.

Nobody was surprised that Brazil, then the best team in the world, won the match, but it did come as a surprise that they only won 4–3. The Irish team had managed to score three times against the reigning world champions.

Every DART user going to city centre from the south would have known Lansdowne Road Stadium from passing it. From Lansdowne Road DART

Lansdowne Stadium
from the air, *c.* 1990.
(Courtesy of Gerard Siggins)

Part of Lansdowne Road
Stadium from the DART
station, 2006.

Station, the stadium presented a view of spectacular ugliness. Keith Wood, a former captain of the Irish rugby team, described it during the opening ceremony of the new stadium: '… a monument in grey … a truly horrible place empty'.[111]

Until and including the first years of this century, whenever there was a match or concert in Lansdowne Road Stadium, DART trains did not stop either at Lansdowne Road or at Sandymount from a certain time before the match or concert until a given time after the event's end. When Grand Canal Dock Station was opened in 2001 the rule applied to that station as well. The reason was probably that the authorities were afraid that masses of people getting off stations near the stadium might cause disturbances on roads and level crossings or that people would be pushed into the water at Grand Canal Dock.

Destruction and re-erection

In the summer of 2006, everything still looked fine, the sun shone onto the pitch and the grass had to be cut.

The final match in Lansdowne Road Stadium was played on 31 December 2006, Leinster against Ulster, in pouring rain; a fitting end to a

Lansdowne Road Stadium, summer 2006.

stadium in which the first match, exactly 130 years earlier, in December 1876, had also been Leinster against Ulster, also in pouring rain. Leinster won both matches, in 1876 with one goal and one try to two tries; in 2006 the score was 20–12. The very last try in the old stadium was scored by Jamie Heaslip for Leinster.

During the next summer, things still did not look too bad, despite the building machinery behind the East Stand.

And then suddenly everything disappeared.

The final bits of the old Lansdowne Road Stadium were removed and the ground levelled.

East Stand, July 2007.

The last remains: Lansdowne Road, September 2007.

Levelled: Lansdowne Road, end of September 2007.

Nothing was left except a model showing what the future might look like. Laying the foundations took time. It was nearly a year before something started to grow upwards.

Model of a section of the Aviva Stadium.

New beginnings: Lansdowne Road, July 2008.

The Lansdowne Road building site from Ringsend, November 2008.

Lansdowne Road from Sandymount Station, January 2009.

Lansdowne Road Stadium from the DART, April 2009.

Aviva Stadium from Sandymount Station, February 2010.

During the years of building the Aviva Stadium, the site was visible from afar because of the building cranes. In the first of those years, trains did not run past the building site on some weekends as the platform for the Lansdowne Lane entrance of the stadium, which bridges the railway line, was being built. Finally, late in 2008, something was taking shape on the old site.

Three months later, anybody waiting for the DART at Sandymount Station could see something looming up from the site.

In February 2010, the roof was finished. The building looked massive, even when seen from Sandymount Station, 750m away.

Aviva Stadium from the DART,
March 2010.

AVIVA – the new Lansdowne Road Stadium

The new stadium was finished on time and within budget; it was built re-using as much as possible from the old structure. To optimise the available space, the pitch axis was turned 15°, compared to that of the old stadium. Such a turn had already been performed during the lifetime of its founder, H.W.D. Dunlop.

Some statistical data: the stadium is 203m long, nearly 190m wide and almost 48m high. All of the 51,000 seats are under the roof. The costs were less than half the costs of the new Wembley Stadium. Wembley is nearly twice the size, but even comparing the price per seat the Aviva was cheaper than Wembley.

Aviva has a natural pitch of dwarf rye grass with a 30cm root zone of elastic band and fibre as the turf has to suffer 19-stone bodies digging in for scrums, but it also has to have a cushion effect when players hit the ground after tackles.[112]

From the top row in the Aviva Stadium, there are spectacular views across the whole pitch and further, past the lower Havelock Square end, right into the north side of Dublin towards Drumcondra.

Aviva Stadium, looking north into Dublin over the Havelock Square end.

Section of the roof of the Aviva Stadium.

From the same viewpoint, it is also easy to study the details of the roof construction.

The new stadium is state-of-the-art all over, including the parts that spectators normally do not see, like the changing rooms, which are spacious. The Aviva Stadium breaks with an old tradition, though: in general, the changing and showering quarters for the guest team are smaller than those for the home team. This is not so in the Aviva. The main reason that both sets of facilities are of the same size is that the new stadium will see matches that do not include Irish teams; for those matches, there will be no 'home' team.

The briefing room not only has normal seats, but also physiotherapy beds, so that players with minor injuries can listen to the coach during the interval.

The shower room is one big room for the whole team. There are exactly fifteen shower heads, one for each member of a regular rugby team, but without any facilities for substitutions.

Adjoining the shower room of the home team is a hydrotherapy room with two basins, one for cold water of 4°C, the other for water of 36°C and underwater jets.

Aviva Stadium, changing room.

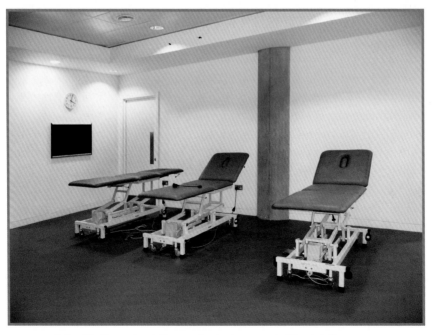

Aviva Stadium, physiotherapy beds at one end of the briefing room.

Aviva Stadium, shower room.

Aviva Stadium, hydrotherapy room.

The medical suite for the teams includes a dentist's chair and an X-ray room.

The complex has three restaurants, sixty bars and food outlets, and nine kitchens with forty-eight chefs, as well as conference facilities with first-aid rooms.

The studios for radio and TV transmission are on the same level as the corporate boxes whereas the media room for newspaper journalists is downstairs with full internet access.

Like most other modern stadia, the Aviva Stadium shows its name on the outside but for international soccer matches, FIFA and UEFA insist on a neutral name. In these situations the words 'Aviva Stadium' are covered up and 'Dublin Arena' is shown instead.

One of the problems the architects of this stadium were faced with was how to evade overshadowing for the residents of Havelock Square and O'Connell Gardens. Their solution was to make the north end of the stadium different from the south end (see photograph on page 144).

The first match in the new stadium was a match between a combined team of young players from Leinster and Ulster against a combined team of Munster and Connaught players, so Leinster and Ulster were involved again. And so was the rain, but this time at least it was showers instead

RTÉ studio in the Aviva Stadium.

Aviva Stadium as seen from Grand Canal Dock DART Station.

Aviva Stadium, north end (Havelock Square side), 31 July 2010, during the first ever match there.

Try by Tom Court, Ireland v. Italy in the Six Nations Championship, 25 February 2012.

Jonathan Sexton converting Tom Court's try.

of a downpour. There were sunny spells as well. The first try scored in the new stadium goes on the account of Craig Gilroy from Ulster; the first conversion after that was successfully managed by Paddy Jackson, also from Ulster. A few years later, both of them and their Leinster teammate Marty Moore were capped for the Irish national team.

Since then the Aviva Stadium has seen many national and international matches.

Appendix

Some Olympians with connections to Pembroke Township/Dublin 4:

1896:   John Pius Boland: gold in tennis single, gold in tennis double (together with Friedrich Traun of Germany). He was a member of the family who owned Boland's Flour Mills in Ringsend.

1908:   James Cecil Parke: silver in tennis men's double. He played rugby for Dublin University and Monkstown, was capped ten times for Leinster between 1901 and 1908 and twenty times for Ireland between 1903 and 1909.

1912:   Ralph Jack Richard Mecredy participated in the 1912 Olympics, cycling in single and team races (team Ireland 3). He lived in Gilford Road for some time.

1920:   Noel Mary Purcell: gold in water polo (for GB). Apart from water polo, he played rugby for Lansdowne FC and was four times capped for Ireland.

1924:   Noel Mary Purcell: captained the Irish water polo team, which included James Beckett, who played rugby for Old Wesley. John Lea and Robert Cowzer of Shelbourne FC were part of the Irish Olympic soccer team.

1948:   Patrick Joseph Duffy was a member of the Irish fencing team.

1952:   Patrick Joseph Duffy was a member of the Irish fencing team. (In the same year he founded Salle d'Armes Duffy.) Brothers Andrew (Ando) and Thomas (Tommy) Reddy of Sandymount Boxing Club were members of the Irish Olympic boxing team.

1956: Ronald Michael Delany: gold medal in 1,500m in Melbourne. Ronnie was a member of Crusaders Athletics Club and Claremont Lawn Tennis Club. For some time, he lived in Sandymount.

1960: Shirley Armstrong was a member of the Irish fencing team, one of only two Irish women in those Olympic Games. She later married Patrick J. Duffy. Andrew (Ando) Reddy of Sandymount Boxing Club was a member of the Irish Olympic Boxing team.

1964: John Bouchier-Hayes and Michael Ryan were members of the Irish Olympic fencing team. They were pupils of Patrick Joseph Duffy.

1968: John Bouchier-Hayes, Fionbarr Farrell, Colm O'Brien and Michael Ryan were members of the Irish Olympic fencing team, all of them pupils of Patrick Joseph Duffy.

1972: John Bouchier-Hayes was the only representative for Ireland in fencing.

1972 and 1976: Mary Purcell of Crusaders AC was a member of the Irish Olympic team for the middle-distance runs.

1972– 1980: Michael Morris, 3rd Baron Killanin, was president of the IOC (International Olympic Committee) from 1972 until 1980. Lord Killanin was married to a granddaughter of Henry Doveton Wallace Dunlop of Lansdowne Road Stadium fame. He lived with his family in Lansdowne Road.

Sources and Further Reading

A Celebration and Commemoration of 100 Years, 2004 Centenary Brochure
(Railway Union Sports Club, Sandymount, 2004)

Armitage, Ernest, *Wesley College Dublin 1845–1995: An Illustrated History*
(Dublin: Wesley College, 1995)

Ball, Francis Elrington, *An Historical Sketch of the Pembroke Township*
(Dublin: Alex Thom & Co. Ltd, 1907)

Bowden, Brian (ed.), *200 Years of a Future Through Education: A History of the Masonic Girls' School* (Dublin: Masonic Girls' Benefit Fund, 1992)

Bowen, Rowland, *Cricket: A History of its Growth & Development Throughout the World*
(London: Eyre & Spottiswoode, 1970)

Brayden, W.H. (ed.), *Royal Dublin Society Bi-Centenary Souvenir 1731–1931* (Dublin: RDS, 1931)

Carroll, Noel, *Sport in Ireland* (Dublin: Department of Foreign Affairs, 1979)

Clanna Gael-Fontenoy: The History of Dublin's GAA Club, Volume I, 1887–1950
(Dublin: Cumann Clanna Gael-Fontenoy, 1995)

Conroy, J.C. (ed.), *Rugby in Leinster 1879–1979* (Dublin: The Centenary Sub-Committee of the Leinster Branch IRFU, 1979)

Cronin, Ciaran, *The Ireland Rugby Miscellany* (London: Vision Sports Publishing, 2007)

Davis, Richard, *Irish Cricket and Nationalism*. Available at: <http://library.la84.org/
SportsLibrary/SportingTraditions/1994/st1002/st1002j.pdf>

de Búrca, Marcus, *Michael Cusack and the GAA* (Dublin: Anvil Books, 1989)

de Courcy, John W., *The Liffey in Dublin* (Dublin: Gill & Macmillan, 1996)

Doran, Beatrice, *Donnybrook: A History* (Dublin: The History Press Ireland, 2013)

Farmar, A. & A. (ed.), *Celebrating 25 Years: Sportsco 1979–2004* (Dublin: Sportsco, 2004)

Foster, Ian (ed.), *Irish Sport 1950–2000* (London: Manticore Books, 2002)

Garnham, Neal, *Association Football and Society in Pre-partition Ireland* (Belfast: Ulster Historical Foundation, 2004)

Gibney, John, 'Green is the Colour' *History Ireland*, Volume 20, No. 5 (Dublin, September/
October 2012)

Goggins, Robert, 'A Brief History of Shamrock Rovers'. Available at:
<www.shamrockrovers.ie/history>

Griffin, Brian, *Cycling in Victorian Ireland* (Dublin: Nonsuch Publishing, 2006)

Hart, Antonia, *Ghost Signs of Dublin* (Dublin: The History Press Ireland, 2014)

King, Séamus J., *A History of Hurling* (Dublin: Gill & Macmillan, 2005)

Lane, Fintan, *Long Bullets: History of Road Bowling in Ireland* (Cork: Galley Head Press, 2005)

Lansdowne FC, *Centenary Year History* (Dublin, 1972)

Lewis, Samuel, *The Topographical Dictionary of Ireland* (London: S. Lewis & Co., 1837)

MacCarthy, R.B. and Paterson, John, *Saint Mark's: The History of a Dublin Parish* (Dublin, 1971)

McKenna, Denis (ed.), *A Social and Natural History of Sandymount Irishtown Ringsend* (Dublin: Sandymount Community Services, 1993)

Maguire, Ashling (ed.), *Donnybrook Lawn Tennis Club 1893–1993* (Dublin, 1993)

Milne, Kenneth, *S. Bartholomew's: A History of the Dublin Parish* (Dublin: Allen Figgis, 1963)

Murray, K.A., *Ireland's First Railway* (Dublin: Irish Railway Record Society, 1981)

O'Connor, Ulick, *Oliver St John Gogarty: A Poet and His Times* (London: NEL Mentor, 1967)

Ó Maitiú, Séamas, *Dublin's Suburban Towns 1834–1930* (Dublin: Four Courts Press, 2003)

O'Neill, Ciaran, *Catholics of Consequence: Transnational Education, Social Mobility and the Irish Catholic Elite 1850–1900* (Oxford: Oxford University Press, 2014)

Peter, A., *Dublin Fragments Social and Historic* (Dublin: Hodges, Figgis & Co., 1927)

Poyntz, S.G., *St. Stephen's: One Hundred and Fifty Years or Worship and Witness* (1974)

Puirséal, Pádraig, *The GAA in its Time* (Swords: Ward River Press, 1984)

Ryan, Christopher, *Lewis' Dublin: A Topographical Dictionary of the Parishes, Towns and Villages of Dublin City and County* (Dublin: The Collins Press, 2001)

Sands, Christopher, 'Our Earlier Champions' available at: <www.shelbournefc.ie>

Saunders, Barry and Bradshaw, David, *Sandymount* (Dublin: Sandymount Association of Youth, 1975)

Siggins, Gerard and Clerkin, Malachy, *Lansdowne Road* (Dublin: The O'Brien Press, 2010)

Somerville-Large, Peter, *Dublin – The First Thousand Years* (Belfast: The Appletree Press, 1988)

The Old Pembroke Township 1863–1930 (Dublin: City of Dublin Vocational Education Committee, 1993 and 2011)

The Origin and Development of Football in Ireland. Being a reprint of R.M. Peter's Irish Football Annual of 1880. With an Introduction by Neal Garnham (Belfast: Ulster Historical Foundation, 1999)

Van Esbeck, Edmund, *The Story of Irish Rugby* (London Stanley Paul & Co., 1986)

Van Esbeck, Edmund, *Old Wesley Rugby Football Club. A Centenary History* (Dublin: Old Wesley RFC, 1991)

Wanderers FC, *Wanderers Football Club 1869/70-1969/70* (Dublin, 1970)

Notes

1   *The Old Township of Pembroke 1863–1930* (Dublin: City of Dublin Vocational Education Committee, 1993), p. 19
2   *Ibid.*, p. 20
3   Peter Somerville-Large, *Dublin – The First Thousand Years* (Belfast: The Appletree Press, 1988)
4   Rowland Bowen, *Cricket: A History of its Growth & Development Throughout the World* (London: Eyre & Spottiswoode, 1970)
5   Séamus J. King, *A History of Hurling* (Dublin: Gill & Macmillan, 2005), p. 19
6   <http://phoenixcricketclub.com/club-life/history/> (accessed August 2014).
7   *The Origin and Development of Football in Ireland. Being a reprint of R. M. Peter's Irish Football Annual of 1880. With an Introduction by Neal Garnham* (Belfast: Ulster Historical Foundation, 1999), p. 48
8   Gerard Siggins & Malachy Clerkin: *Lansdowne Road* (Dublin: The O'Brien Press, 2010)
9   *Centenary Year History* (Lansdowne FC, 1972), p. 9
10 Antonia Hart, *Ghost Signs of Dublin* (Dublin: The History Press Ireland, 2014)
11 *A Celebration and Commemoration of 100 years 1904–2004: Club History* (Dublin: The Railway Union & Steampacket Athletic & Social Union, 2004), p. 5
12 Marcus de Búrca, *Michael Cusack and the GAA* (Dublin: Anvil Books, 1989)
13 Shay Connolly, 'The Fontenoy Files' in *News Four* (June 2007)
14 Marcus de Búrca, *Michael Cusack and the GAA* (Dublin: Anvil Books, 1989)
15 Printed in *Clanna Gael-Fontenoy: The History of Dublin's GAA Club*, Volume 1, 1887–1950 (Dublin 1994), p. 28
16 <http://clannagaelfontenoy.ie/?page_id=57> (accessed March 2015)
17 *Freeman's Journal*, 24 October 1879, as quoted in: J.C. Conroy: *Rugby in Leinster 1879–1979* (Dublin: Leinster Branch IRFU, 1979)
18 W.Bro. Dr Brian Bowden (ed.), *200 Years of a Future Through Education: A History of the Masonic Girls' Charity* (Dublin: Masonic Girls Benefit Fund, 1992)
19 <http://en.wikipedia.org/wiki/John_Pius_Boland> (accessed April 2015)
20 <www.historyireland.com/20th-century-contemporary-history/john-pius-bolands-olympic-tennis-diploma/> (accessed February 2015)
21 'From the Archives', 4 October 1954. *The Irish Times*, Tuesday, 4 October 2011
22 Francis Elrington Ball, *An Historical Sketch of the Pembroke Township* (Dublin: Alex. Thom & Co., 1907), p. 32
23 Murray, K.A., *Ireland's First Railway* (Dublin: Irish Railway Record Society, 1981)
24 W.Bro. Dr Brian Bowden (ed.), *200 Years of a Future Through Education: A History of the*

Masonic Girls' Charity (Dublin: Masonic Girls Benefit Fund, 1992)

25   *Wanderers Football Club* 1869/70 1969/70, p. 11

26   *Ibid*, p. 9

27   *The Origin and Development of Football in Ireland. Being a reprint of R.M. Peter's Irish Football Annual of 1880. With an Introduction by Neal Garnham* (Belfast: Ulster Historical Foundation, 1999)

28   Garry Redmond, 'Our Neighbours'; in *Wanderers Football Club* 1869/70 1969/70, p. 83 (quoted with permission of Wanderers FC)

29   J.C. Conroy (ed.), *Rugby in Leinster 1879-1979* (Dublin: The Centenary Sub-Committee of the Leinster Branch IRFU, 1979)

30   *The Origin and Development of Football in Ireland. Being a reprint of R.M. Peter's Irish Football Annual of 1880. With an Introduction by Neal Garnham* (Belfast: Ulster Historical Foundation, 1999), p. 89

31   *Ibid.*

32   <www.bectiverangers.com> (accessed March 2015)

33   *The Origin and Development of Football in Ireland. Being a reprint of R.M. Peter's Irish Football Annual of 1880. With an Introduction by Neal Garnham* (Belfast: Ulster Historical Foundation, 1999), p. 89

34   *Ibid.*

35   Ernest Armitage, *Wesley College Dublin 1845–1995* (Dublin: Wesley College, 1995)

36   Edmund van Esbeck: *Old Wesley Rugby Football Club: A Centenary History 1891–1991* (Dublin: Old Wesley RFC, 1991), p. 5

37   *Ibid.* p. 32

38   <www.leinsterrugby.ie/branch/about/index.php> (accessed March 2015)

39   Edmund van Esbeck, *The Story of Irish Rugby* (London: Stanley Paul & Co., 1986)

40   J.C. Conroy (ed.), *Rugby in Leinster 1879–1979* (Dublin: The Centenary Sub-Committee of the Leinster Branch IRFU, 1979)

41   Many thanks to Gerard Siggins for this suggestion.

42   Richard Davis: *Irish Cricket and Nationalism*. Available at: <http://library.la84.org/SportsLibrary/SportingTraditions/1994/st1002/st1002j.pdf> (accessed March 2015).

43   Gerard Siggins & Malachy Clerkin, *Lansdowne Road* (Dublin: The O'Brien Press, 2010)

44   *Ibid.*

45   Beatrice M. Doran, *Donnybrook: A History* (Dublin: The History Press Ireland, 2013)

46   <www.nationalarchives.ie/PDF/PembrokeEstatePapers.pdf> (accessed February 2015)

47   Clanna Gael-Fontenoy, *The History of Dublin's GAA Club*, Volume I, 1887–1950 (Dublin, 1994), p. 94

48   <http://clannagaelfontenoy.ie> (accessed February 2015)

49   Ciaran O'Neill, *Catholics of Consequence: Transnational Education, Social Mobility and the Irish Catholic Elite 1850–1900* (Oxford: Oxford University Press, 2014)

50   <www.youtube.com/watch?v=i3i6mGoXT6o&feature=player_embedded> (accessed Augusts 2015)

51   Review of *Talking History: A History of Shamrock Rovers* in *History Ireland*, Vol. 20, No. 6, Nov/Dec 2012, p. 48

52   <www.shamrockrovers.ie/history> (accessed March 2015)

53   R.B. MacCarthy and John Paterson, *Saint Mark's: The History of a Dublin Parish* (Dublin, 1971)

54   S.G. Poyntz, *Saint Stephen's: One Hundred and Fifty Years of Worship and Witness* (Dublin, 1974)

55   R.B. MacCarthy and John Paterson, *Saint Mark's: The History of a Dublin Parish* (Dublin, 1971)

56   Neal Garnham, *Association Football and Society in Pre-partition Ireland* (Belfast: Ulster Historical Foundation, 2004)

57   <www.rsssf.com/tablesn/nilhist.html> (accessed February 2015)

58   <www.soccer-ireland.com/dublin-football-clubs/liffeys-pearse-fc.htm> (accessed March 2015)

59   <www.ddda.ie/files/publications/docs/newsletterissue13.pdf> (accessed March 2015)

60   Gerard Siggins & Malachy Clerkin, *Lansdowne Road* (Dublin: The O'Brien Press, 2010), p. 55

61   <www.lansdowneltc.com/same/history.htm> (accessed March 2015).

62   Ashling Maguire (ed.), *Donnybrook Lawn Tennis Club 1893–1993* (Dublin, 1993)

63   Kenneth Milne, *S. Bartholomew's: A History of the Dublin Parish* (Dublin: Allen Figgis, 1963)

64   S.G. Poyntz, *St. Stephen's: One Hundred and Fifty Years or Worship and Witness* (1974)

65   Different spellings exist for this family name: Frensche, Frensch, ffrench, Ffrench and French

66   Samuel Lewis, *The Topographical Dictionary of Ireland* (London: S. Lewis & Co., 1837)

67   Thomas Butler, 6th Earl of Ossory stood in as deputy for his father James Butler, 1st Duke of Ormonde who was Lord Lieutenant at that time

68   *Pue's Occurrences*, 7 September 1771.

69   Brian Griffin, *Cycling in Victorian Ireland* (Dublin: Nonsuch Publishing, 2006)

70   *Ibid.*

71   Obituary in the *British Medical Journal*, 21 May 1921, 1(3151): 760

72   <http://homepage.eircom.net/~thevets/henryprofile.htm>

73   Noel Carroll, *Sport in Ireland* (Dublin: Department of Foreign Affairs, 1979)

74   *Ibid.*

75   Marcus de Búrca, *Michael Cusack and the GAA* (Dublin: Anvil Books, 1989)

76   Denis McKenna (ed.), *A Social and Natural History of Sandymount Irishtown Ringsend* (Dublin: Sandymount Community Services, 1993)

77   <http://hear-the-boat-sing.blogspot.ie/2011/05/more-irish-rowing.html> (accessed August 2014).

78   <www.inarchive.com/ie/d/dublin.ie/746095/2011–08–07–description/80/Sandymouny_Boxing_club_off_Pearse_Street/> (accessed February 2015)

79   <http://familytreemaker.genealogy.com/users/m/u/r/William-Thomas-Murphy-Leinster/WEBSITE-0001/UHP-0105.html> (and equivalent other persons of that family) (accessed February 2015)

80   ADFD = *Akademie der Fechtkunst Deutschlands*, AAI = *Académie d'Armes Internationale*, AAF = *Académie d'Armes de France*

81   <www.pembrokefencing.ie> (accessed February 2015)

82   Peter Somerville-Large, *Dublin. The First Thousand Years* (Belfast: The Appletree Press, 1988)

83   A. Peter, *Dublin Fragments Social and Historic* (Dublin: Hodges, Figgis & Co., 1925), p. 17

84   <www.esbsc.com/abouts-us/> (accessed March 2015)

85   <www.tcdlife.ie/clubs/boat/history.php> (accessed March 2015)

86   *The Origin and Development of Football in Ireland. Being a reprint of R. M. Peter's Irish Football Annual of 1880. With an Introduction by Neal Garnham* (Belfast: Ulster Historical Foundation, 1999), p. 21

87   <www.duboatclub.com/about-dubc/> (accessed March 2015)

88   <www.malahideheritage.com/#!portregattas/c20r> (accessed March 2015)

89   <www.tcdlife.ie/clubs/boat/history.php> (accessed March 2015)

90   <http://hear-the-boat-sing.blogspot.ie/2011/08/dublin-rowing-club-1906-1942-part1.html>

and <http://hear-the-boat-sing.blogspot.ie/2011/08/greg-denieffe-story-of-dublin-rowing.html> (accessed October 2014)

91 Denis McKenna (ed.), *The Roads to Sandymount Irishtown Ringsend* (Dublin: Sandymount Community Services, 1996)

92 <http://ucdbc.ie/index.php/history/rowing-available-at-one-penny-fare-from-dolier-st/> (accessed March 2015)

93 *Clanna Gael-Fontenoy: The History of Dublin's GAA Club*, Volume I, 1887–1950 (Dublin, 1994), p. 47

94 <www.ucd.ie/archaeology/documentstore/hc_reports/lod/Ringsend_Park_Final.pdf> (accessed March 2015)

95 <www.irishlawnbowls.ie/mhistory.html> (accessed March 2015)

96 <www.ucd.ie/archaeology/documentstore/hc_reports/lod/Herbert_Park_final.pdf> (accessed March 2015)

97 <https://dublinsportsarchive.wordpress.com/2011/05/03/marks-story/#more-77> (accessed January 2015).

98 *Ibid.*

99 <https://radicalmanchester.wordpress.com/2009/08/24/paddy-o%E2%80%99donoghue/> (accessed March 2015)

100 <www.youtube.com/watch?v=VM8ArZ3o8qE> (accessed Nov 2014)

101 <http://bectiverangers.com/about/3841-2/> (accessed March 2015)

102 Edmund van Elsbeck, *Old Wesley Rugby Football Club. A Centenary History 1891–1991* (Dublin, 1991), p. 26

103 J.C. Conroy (ed.), *Rugby in Leinster 1879–1979* (Dublin: The Centenary Sub-Committee of the Leinster Branch IRFU, 1979)

104 <http://articles.chicagotribune.com/2012-08-31/sports/ct-spt-0901-prep-foot-loyola-dublin_1_peter-pujals-julius-holley-loyola> (accessed Nov 2014)

105 <www.jjon.org/jioyce-s-people/conneff> (accessed March 2015)

106 W.H. Brayden (ed.), *Royal Dublin Society Bi-Centenary Souvenir 1731–1931* (Dublin, 1931)

107 <www.rugbyfootballhistory.com/lansdowne.html> (accessed January 2015)

108 *Centenary Year History* (Lansdowne Football Club, 1972), p. 9

109 *The Irish Times*, Saturday, 2 May 2015

110 Lansdowne Yesterday: New Projection Project 1978 (Lansdowne, Dublin 1978)

111 *The Irish Times*, Saturday, 15 May 2010

112 *The Sunday Times*, 25 July 2010

Also from The History Press

SPORTING FUN

The History Press Ireland